D1289041

Advance Praise for *1620*

Peter Wood's pushback against the 1619 Project is at once sharp, illuminating, entertaining, and profound. More than a powerful exposé of the 1619 Project's mendacity, Wood's *1620* explains why so many Americans have succumbed to this exercise in manipulation – and shows the way to fight back.

STANLEY KURTZ
senior fellow, Ethics and Public Policy Center

Via Peter Wood, the "civil body politic" of the Mayflower Compact reasserts itself in the national conversation. *1620* is a dispassionate, clear reminder that the best in America's past is still America's best future.

AMITY SHLAES
chair, Calvin Coolidge Presidential Foundation

Peter Wood's *1620* claims the prize as the most comprehensive response to the ill-fated 1619 Project. In a thorough review of the text, Wood accounts for every argument for and against. He appropriately honors the Project's intention to pursue a mission of redress, while nevertheless pinpointing its consistent resort to misrepresentation that cannot be dismissed as merely different interpretation. Wood identifies the heart of the matter: Surely there are ways to incorporate a forthright treatment of slavery, racism, and the black experience into the story of America's rise as a free, self-governing, creative, and prosperous nation. The key to doing that is to put the pursuit of the ideals of liberty and justice at the center of the story. The 1619 Project failed in that for the sufficient reason that its purpose was cultural shakedown, not cultural affirmation. That is made plain in this necessary work.

WILLIAM ALLEN
emeritus dean and professor, Michigan State University

With elegant precision Peter Wood dismantles the edifice ostentatiously called a "reframing" of American history, the 1619 Project. He deftly exposes the jumble of lies, half-lies, logical fallacies, bad history, and bad faith of a project motivated by greed and hatred of America. For anyone who cares about history, education, truth, and the United States of America, *1620* is essential reading.

MARY GRABAR

resident fellow, Alexander Hamilton Institute

Peter Wood's survey of the landscape of scholarly criticism has provided a valuable service, both in assessing the heated historical debates around the 1619 Project and by offering readers an accessible roadmap with which to navigate its many controversies. Unfortunately the *New York Times* has thus far conspicuously avoided the most salient criticisms of its work. This helpful guide masterfully curates the scholarly scrutiny that the newspaper evaded and ignored, equipping the reader to approach the 1619 Project with a discerning eye for evidence-based history.

PHILLIP W. MAGNESS

senior research fellow, American Institute for Economic Research

Those of us who remain attached to the principles of the Founding need to read *1620: A Critical Response to the 1619 Project* with both care and gratitude. For Peter Wood, like a highly trained commando, has advanced to the front lines to clear away the dangerous rubbish put forth by the 1619 Project. With critical skill and in clear prose, he has opened multiple avenues of assault on a misguided enterprise that in trying to rewrite history deserves to end up on its ash-heap.

ROBERT PAQUETTE

president, Alexander Hamilton Institute;
emeritus professor of history, Hamilton College

1620

1620

*A Critical Response
to the 1619 Project*

PETER W. WOOD

ENCOUNTER BOOKS
NEW YORK · LONDON

© 2020 by Peter W. Wood

All rights reserved. No part of this publication may be reproduced, stored in a retrieval system, or transmitted, in any form or by any means, electronic, mechanical, photocopying, recording, or otherwise, without the prior written permission of Encounter Books, 900 Broadway, Suite 601, New York, New York, 10003.

First American edition published in 2020 by Encounter Books, an activity of Encounter for Culture and Education, Inc., a nonprofit, tax exempt corporation.
Encounter Books website address: www.encounterbooks.com

Manufactured in the United States and printed on acid-free paper. The paper used in this publication meets the minimum requirements of ANSI/NISO Z39.48—1992 (R 1997) (*Permanence of Paper*).

FIRST AMERICAN EDITION

LIBRARY OF CONGRESS CATALOGING-IN-PUBLICATION DATA

Names: Wood, Peter, 1953– author.
Title: 1620 : a critical response to the 1619 Project / Peter W. Wood.
Other titles: Critical response to the 1619 Project
Description: New York, NY : Encounter Books, [2020] | Includes bibliographical references and index. |
Identifiers: LCCN 2020032266 (print) | LCCN 2020032267 (ebook) | ISBN 9781641771245 (cloth) | ISBN 9781641771252 (ebook)
Subjects: LCSH: Slavery—United States—History. | United States—History—Study and teaching. | 1619 Project. | United States—Historiography. | Critical pedagogy.
Classification: LCC E441.W873 2020 (print) | LCC E441 (ebook) | DDC 306.3/620973—dc23
LC record available at https://lccn.loc.gov/2020032266
LC ebook record available at https://lccn.loc.gov/2020032267

CONTENTS

WHAT IS
THE 1619 PROJECT?

O N SUNDAY, August 18, 2019, the *New York Times* published a special issue of *The New York Times Magazine* announcing "The 1619 Project." Along with the 100-page magazine, the *New York Times* released a sixteen-page newsprint section under the same title and headlined "We've Got to Tell the Unvarnished Truth," quoting the late historian John Hope Franklin.

On the opening page of the magazine, Jake Silverstein, the *Times*' editor in chief, stated the project's aim:

> *The goal of The* 1619 *Project, a major initiative from* The New York Times *that this issue of the magazine inaugurates, is to reframe American history by considering what it would mean to regard* 1619 *as our nation's birth year. Doing so requires us to place the consequences of slavery and the contributions of black Americans at the very center of the story we tell ourselves about who we are as a country.*[1]

Reframing the country's history is an extraordinarily ambitious goal, and not something one would ordinarily expect to come from a newspaper. The *Times*, however, is not the least bit circumspect in announcing it. The 1619 Project is, in other words, an all-out effort to replace traditional conceptions of American history with a history refracted through the lens of black identity politics.

This approach goes far beyond the case for teaching African American Studies in colleges or making sure that black history is integrated in school curricula. Instead of asserting the need to *add* to traditional American history a fuller account of the black experience, the 1619 Project calls for *replacing* that traditional account with one that makes the black experience primary – and not just for black Americans, but for all Americans.

This short book responds to the 1619 Project, but it is not a point-by-point examination of everything the contributors to the 1619 Project first wrote or of what they and others have said since. I aim instead to take the reader on a hike through the main themes of the 1619 Project, pointing out the dizzying vistas, treacherous paths, poisonous snakes, sudden drop-offs, and hungry grizzly bears. The central tenets of the 1619 Project are that Americans have grossly misunderstood the origins and nature of American society, and that slavery is the pivotal institution in American history.

The contributors to the 1619 Project are, of course, more specific. Their claims include the idea that America began with the arrival of slaves in Virginia in August 1619; that the primary purpose of the colonists who declared independence from Britain in 1776 was to preserve American slavery from the danger of Britain's outlawing it; that the Southern plantation system of growing cotton with slave labor is the foundation of modern American capitalism; and that Lincoln was a racist who had no interest in conferring real citizenship on those who were enslaved.

What Is the 1619 Project?

The project's contributors undoubtedly knew these to be provocative claims. In their statements and behavior in the months that followed the release of the special issue of the magazine, some of them relished both the adulation they received from supporters and the dismay of critics, who proved ineffectual in stemming public attention to the *Times'* splash.

It quickly became clear that the 1619 Project was a lot more than the initial publication of the magazine and the newspaper supplement. It was and still is a "project" in the fullest sense of the term. The Pulitzer Center partnered with the *Times* to plant a 1619 Project curriculum in the nation's schools. Nikole Hannah-Jones, the architect of the 1619 Project and author of its lead essay, went on a nationwide speaking tour and was met by friendly audiences. The *Times* not only heavily advertised the project, it seeded themes from the project in hundreds of news stories and columns. It added a podcast devoted to the project, and it used its weekly online newsletter, "Race/Related," to stoke the fire. Given the *Times'* status as the nation's "newspaper of record" and the lodestar for other news organizations, 1619 Project themes and conceits began to appear everywhere in the nation's press, with or without explicit mention of the project itself.

The larger aim of the 1619 Project is to change America's understanding of itself. Whether it will ultimately succeed in doing so remains to be seen, but it certainly has already succeeded in shaping how Americans now argue about key aspects of our history. The 1619 Project aligns with the views of those on the progressive left who hate America and would like to transform it radically into a different kind of nation. Such a transformation would be a terrible mistake: it would endanger our hard-won liberty, our self-government, and our virtues as a people. Little is to be gained, however, by progressives and conservatives lobbing boulder-sized principles back and forth across the line that divides them.

Instead, this book explores the 1619 Project as a cultural phenomenon: a testimony to the beliefs and ambitions of one faction. That I do not share these beliefs and ambitions gives me the freedom to consider them from angles that the project's adherents might not entertain. That freedom also allows me to examine criticisms of the 1619 Project coming from many whose premises I don't share: hard-core Marxists, liberal statists, hard-core free-market advocates, and Southern apologists, among others. My own views, which I have presented in other books and articles, are of a mildly conservative and traditionalist sort. I regard the primary values of our nation as stated clearly in the second paragraph of the Declaration of Independence, namely, "that all men are created equal, that they are endowed by their Creator with certain unalienable Rights, that among these are Life, Liberty and the pursuit of Happiness. – That to secure these rights, Governments are instituted among Men, deriving their just powers from the consent of the governed."

On matters of race, I uphold the principle that our Constitution and our laws should be colorblind, and that our society should strive for the common good, which is best achieved by treating one another as individuals, not as representatives of identity groups. We do, however, have the freedom to form our own communities and to enjoy shared cultural affinities. "Race" in that sense is not likely to disappear anytime soon in a general cultural amalgamation. People will separate and divide themselves as often as people will "appropriate" from the cultural traditions of others. There is nothing sinister in either impulse.

What Is the 1619 Project?

But this leaves open the question of how racist and how oppressive American society really is. I believe there is abundant exaggeration on both left and right, much of it driven by politics. Some exaggerate the degree to which racism pervades American society. Some exaggerate the degree to which racism is a thing of the past that contemporary America has moved beyond. It is very difficult for most Americans to avoid exaggerating in one direction or the other. If you have experienced overt racism or seen it up close, it is likely to loom very large in your assessment of the nation. If you have not experienced racism first-hand, it is likely to appear to you to be merely a talking point for those who cling to a particular narrative, when they could just as easily enjoy the full freedoms that the country offers. Who is right?

The 1619 Project offers the fullest and most vigorous exposition of the view that America is a racist, oppressive country. Fringe groups of black nationalists take an even grimmer view, but the 1619 Project has taken ideas that a few years ago were exclusively fringe a good way into the realm of mainstream opinion. The idea, for example, that the American Revolution was a pro-slavery event once circulated only among conspiracy-minded activists with comic-book-style theories of history. The 1619 Project has brought it from the playground into the classroom, to the consternation of serious historians everywhere.

Slavery, of course, was not an American invention, or a European one. It has existed in human societies for thousands of years. In north and east Africa, slave capture and trading were pursued on an enormous scale by Arabs. When Europeans encountered native kingdoms on Africa's Atlantic coast in the fifteenth century, they discovered slavery as a deeply embedded practice. That the Portuguese and the Spanish fostered this practice by creating a market for African slaves in the New World is among the great tragedies of human history. Other European powers eventually joined in perpetuating that tragedy.

By comparison with the Caribbean and South American colonies, the English colonies that would one day become the United States were lightly touched by the slave trade, especially during their first hundred years. The 1619 Project argues to the contrary that the enslavement of Africans was central to the formation of American social order and the American economy as early as the seventeenth century.

The usual way for disputes about history to be resolved is for historians to present their best arguments, and their sources, in journal articles; each side can then examine the evidence for themselves and hammer out the truth. The 1619 Project evades this kind of transparency. The lead author, Nikole Hannah-Jones, who makes some of the most audacious claims, cites no sources at all: the project as presented in the magazine contains no footnotes, bibliography, or other scholarly footholds.

An ordinary reader would not expect such things in a Sunday newspaper, but the 1619 Project is not an ordinary piece of newspaper journalism. It is an attempt to wrest control of the grand narrative of American history. That really isn't the proper role for a newspaper, which should report the news rather than attempt to create it. The *Times* stumbled badly by presenting unsourced and unsupported assertions as the writing of history. Much of the controversy that followed consisted of historians' challenging the claims and the *Times*' scrambling to find some plausible substantiating evidence.

I chose the title *1620* mainly as a riposte to the claim

What Is the 1619 Project?

that the arrival of slaves in Virginia was the real founding of America. In November 1620, the passengers on the *Mayflower* drew up an agreement on how they would conduct their public affairs when they disembarked. That document, the Mayflower Compact, I argue – as have many others – pointed the way toward America's self-government. It is the beginning of ordered liberty in the New World. That is the vantage point from which I survey the 1619 Project. America was never a "slavocracy." It was and is humanity's great attempt to create a society based on principles of freedom and equality.

This book, I repeat, does not respond to every component of the 1619 Project, but only to the pieces that I judge to be central or most representative of the whole. The hike on which I lead you will not cover every inch of the Grand Tetons, just the best and the scariest parts. The reader may find it helpful, however, to have a map of the project in its entirety.

The August 18 *New York Times Magazine* presented thirty-six separately bylined contributions. Ten of these are articles of several pages, and one is a multipage photo-essay. Eight are brief articles or sidebars. Seventeen are brief literary works commissioned from black writers by the *Times* for this project. Not including the photos in the photo-essay, there are forty stand-alone photographs or artworks of some sort. There is also the cover photo and text, a table of contents, three pages of photos and notes on the contributors, and a pertinent announcement from the Pulitzer Center on the inside back cover.

The longer articles have peculiar, sentence-like titles. They are as follows (the online version of the 1619 Project emends the titles as noted and also presents the articles in a different order):

Preliminaries

1. Nikole Hannah-Jones, "Our democracy's founding ideals of liberty and equality were false when they were written. Black Americans fought to make them true. Without this struggle, America would have no democracy at all." (As emended, "Our democracy's founding ideals were false when they were written. Black Americans have fought to make them true.")

2. Matthew Desmond, "In order to understand the brutality of American capitalism, you have to start on the plantation."

3. Jeneen Interlandi, "Why doesn't the United States have universal health care? The answer begins with policies enacted after the Civil War." (The second part of the title was emended as "The answer has everything to do with race.")

4. Kevin M. Kruse, "A traffic jam in Atlanta would seem to have nothing to do with slavery. But look closer." ("What does a traffic jam in Atlanta have to do with segregation? Quite a lot.")

5. Jamelle Bouie, "American democracy has never shed an undemocratic assumption present at its founding: that some people are inherently entitled to more power than others." ("America holds onto an undemocratic assumption from its founding: that some people deserve more power than others.")

6. Linda Villarosa, "Myths about physical racial differences were used to justify slavery – and are still believed by doctors today."

7. Wesley Morris, "For centuries, black music, forged in bondage, has been the sound of complete artistic freedom. No wonder everybody is always stealing it."

8. Khalil Gibran Muhammad, "The sugar that saturates the American diet has a barbaric history as the 'white gold' that fueled slavery."

9. Bryan Stevenson, "Slavery gave America a fear of black people and a taste for violent punishment. Both still define our criminal-justice system."

10. Trymaine Lee, "A vast wealth gap, driven by segregation, redlining, evictions and exclusion, separates black and white America."

The multipage photo-essay is by Djeneba Aduayom, with accompanying text by Nikole Hannah-Jones and Wadzanai Mhute: "Their ancestors were enslaved by law. Today, they are graduates of the nation's preeminent historically black law school."

These are the short articles (titles as emended in the online version as noted):

1. Jake Silverstein (*Times Magazine* editor in chief), "1619." ("Why We Published the 1619 Project.")

2. Tiya Miles, "Chained Migration: How Slavery Made Its Way West." ("How Slavery Made Its Way West.")

3. Mehrsa Baradaran, "Mortgaging the Future: The North-South rift led to a piecemeal system of bank regulation – with dangerous consequences." ("The Limits of Banking Regulation.")

4. Mehrsa Baradaran, "Good as Gold: In Lincoln's wartime 'greenbacks,' a preview of the 20th-century rise of fiat currency." ("Fiat Currency and the Civil War.")

5. Mehrsa Baradaran, "Fabric of Modernity: How Southern cotton became the cornerstone of a new

global commodities trade." ("Cotton and the Global Market.")

6. Tiya Miles, "Municipal Bonds: How Slavery Built Wall Street." ("How Slavery Made Wall Street.")

7. Tiya Miles, "Pecan Pioneer: The Enslaved Man Who Cultivated the South's Favorite Nut." ("The Enslaved Pecan Pioneer.")

8. Anne C. Bailey, text, with photograph by Dannielle Bowman, "Shadow of the Past."

The literary works, mostly untitled, are by the following writers:

1. Clint Smith (a poem about the arrival of slaves in Virginia in 1619)

2. Yusef Komunyakaa (a poem about the killing of Crispus Attucks, 1770)

3. Eve L. Ewing (a poem about Phillis Wheatley's poems published in 1773)

4. Reginald Dwayne Betts (a graphic about the Fugitive Slave Act of 1793)

5. Barry Jenkins (a prose account of a slave rebellion in Virginia in 1800)

6. Jesmyn Ward (a prose account of the end of importing slaves in 1808)

7. Tyehimba Jess (a poem about the American attack on Negro Fort in 1816)

8. Darryl Pinckney (a prose account of the Emancipation Proclamation, 1863)

9. ZZ Packer (a prose account of a mass killing in Louisiana in 1866)

10. Yaa Gyasi (a prose account of the Tuskegee Study of untreated syphilis, 1932)

11. Jacqueline Woodson (a prose account of the beating of Isaac Woodward, 1946)

12. Rita Dove (a poem about the Ku Klux Klan bombing of the 16th Street Baptist Church, 1963)

13. Camille T. Dungy (a poem also about the Ku Klux Klan bombing of the 16th Street Church)

14. Joshua Bennett (a poem about the founding of the Black Panthers, 1966)

15. Lynn Nottage (a prose account of the first rap song, "Rapper's Delight," 1979)

16. Kiese Laymon (a prose account of Jesse Jackson calling for a Rainbow Coalition, 1984)

17. Clint Smith (a poem about Hurricane Katrina, 2005)

The *Times'* sixteen-page newspaper supplement offers only one substantial essay: Nikita Stewart, "Why Can't We Teach This?" (It is also published in the online version of the magazine as "'We are committing educational malpractice': Why slavery is mistaught – and worse – in American schools," and headlined on the *Times'* website as "Why Can't We Teach Slavery Right in American Schools?")

The rest of the supplement consists of full- and half-page graphics and photographs "curated by Mary Elliott," with text by Mary Elliott and Jazmine Hughes.

Preliminaries

These include images of "an iron ballast block" recovered from a slave ship that sank off the coast of Cape Town in 1794 and of iron shackles for a child (from "before 1860"). Three pages feature short articles, numbered 1 to 3. No. 1 is titled "Slavery, Power and the Human Cost, 1455–1775." No. 2 is titled "The Limits of Freedom, 1776–1808." No. 3 is titled "A Slave Nation Fights for Freedom, 1809–1865."

This material all fits thematically with the 1619 Project, though how exactly it is intended to advance the cause is unclear. Reading the supplement is like walking through a not-so-well-organized museum exhibit that follows rough chronology, and presents some striking images, but is overpowered by one screaming headline after another.

The 1619 Project plainly does not end with these two publications on August 18, 2019. Many more statements followed and are continuing to be issued. But the magazine, and to a lesser extent the newspaper supplement, define the scope of the project and embody its spirit.

It bears noting that the contributors to the 1619 Project are well educated and well placed. Their views may in a general sense be understood as representative of elite education in the United States. Of the fourteen main contributors and the suppliers of sidebars, seven are professional journalists, six of whom work for the *New York Times*. Six are academics, five of whom are historians. One, Bryan Stevenson, is a practicing attorney and noted author.

Nikole Hannah-Jones, journalist (*Times*). BA, University of Notre Dame; MA (journalism), University of North Carolina at Chapel Hill.

Matthew Desmond, sociologist (Princeton). BA, Arizona State University; PhD (sociology), University of Wisconsin.

Jeneen Interlandi, editor (*Times*). BA (biology), Rutgers University; MA and MS (journalism), Columbia University.

Kevin M. Kruse, historian (Princeton). BA, University of North Carolina at Chapel Hill; MA and PhD, Cornell University.

Jamelle Bouie, opinion columnist (*Times*). BA, University of Virginia.

Linda Villarosa, journalist (*Times*). BA, University of Colorado; MA (journalism), City University of New York.

Wesley Morris, journalist (*Times*). BA, Yale University.

Khalil Gibran Muhammad, historian (Harvard). BA (economics), University of Pennsylvania; PhD, Rutgers University.

Bryan Stevenson, attorney. BA, Eastern University; JD, Harvard Law; MA, Kennedy School of Government, Harvard.

Trymaine Lee, journalist (MSNBC). BA, Rowan University.

Jake Silverstein, editor in chief (*Times*). BA (English), Wesleyan University; MA (English), Hollins University; MFA, University of Texas.

Tiya Miles, historian (Harvard). AB, Harvard University; MA, Emory University; PhD, University of Minnesota.

Preliminaries

Mehrsa Baradaran, law professor (University of California at Irvine). BA, Brigham Young University; JD, New York University.

Anne C. Bailey, historian (SUNY Binghamton). AB, Harvard University; MA and PhD, University of Pennsylvania.

This gathering of contributors might not be the ideal panel to reconceive the history of America from the ground up. It looks like there are some significant gaps in their collective knowledge of the country, and perhaps an overemphasis on journalistic approaches. Law, economics, philosophy, the military, the arts, religion, and many other fields are either absent or lightly represented. But this is a mild criticism. The participants weren't invited for the purpose of summoning intellectually diverse views, but because they were known and could be trusted to stay within an agreed-upon framework. They are advocates for a thesis, and it is a thesis that puts racial grievance at the center of America's story.

OCTOBER 1492

WHEN COLUMBUS SET FOOT on Watling's Island in the Bahamas on October 12, 1492, he set in train events that would change the whole world. He was, of course, confused about his location. He imagined himself on the outskirts of Asia, which is about twelve thousand miles west of Watling's Island – half the circumference of the Earth. Scholars believe Columbus erred by relying on old books that estimated latitude in Arab miles, which he mistook for shorter Roman miles.

In September 1999, another long-distance voyage failed for similar reasons. Ten months earlier, NASA had fired off the Mars Climate Orbiter. The $125 million device reached Mars but immediately disintegrated. The design team, led by Lockheed Martin Astronautics, had built the machine using English units of measurement – inches and feet – while the navigation team at the Jet Propulsion Laboratory did its calculations in the metric system.

NASA's accident left a lot of red-faced engineers. Columbus's accident led to Europeans' discovering corn, tomatoes, tobacco, potatoes, sweet potatoes, peppers, pumpkins, peanuts, vanilla, blueberries, and chocolate among some ninety New World crops. These were part of what is now called the Columbian Exchange. Material

Preface

items flowed in both directions. The New World peoples soon had rice, citrus fruits, and bananas brought by Europeans – and exotic animals including horses, donkeys, mules, pigs, cattle, sheep, goats, chickens, cats, and larger breeds of dogs. Europeans also introduced Western technology, including wheeled vehicles and more advanced metallurgy.

These days Columbus is more often excoriated than he is celebrated. His accusers emphasize that native peoples had little immunity to the diseases that Europeans brought with them, and the death rates from the resulting epidemics were appalling. Moreover, in the wake of Columbus's discoveries came brutal Spanish adventurers intent on coercing labor and extracting every bit of wealth they could from the local inhabitants. Columbus, in fact, and at least some Spanish clerics and officials, tried hard to protect native people but failed to impede the demographic disaster that followed contact. They also could not stop the orgy of rape, murder, and plunder, documented by the Dominican friar Bartolomé de las Casas in a series of reports – giving rise to the "Black Legend" of Spanish cruelty in the New World.[1] The Spanish, and soon the Portuguese, saw the opportunity to impose forced labor on the natives. Slavery, first in the mines and soon on plantations, became part of the Columbian Exchange.

Slavery itself, however, was nothing new to the New World. It was an institution familiar to many native societies in both North and South America. These populations had been enslaving one another, as far as we can tell, from time immemorial, and forced labor was far from the worst of it. Captured people fed the almost industrial level of human sacrifice at the center of the Aztec Empire. Some New World peoples captured and kept their enemies for rituals and the sport of torture and, in the case of cannibalistic societies, to maintain a mobile food supply. Cortés could not have captured Tenochtitlán without the aid of tens of thousands of indigenous allies who had been suffering under the Aztecs' brutal imperial rule.

As Europeans learned of these hideous customs, they were relieved of any qualms they had about extracting labor from or forcing Christian conversion on the people they encountered. Better to have your beating heart ripped out of your chest by a masked man with an obsidian knife, or to kneel to a painted image of the Virgin Mary?

Native peoples saw the Europeans as fair game for slavery as well. We have, for example, the account of Álvar Núñez Cabeza de Vaca, a Spanish nobleman and would-be conquistador who served as the treasurer of the ill-fated Narváez Expedition in 1528. De Vaca and some three hundred compatriots intended to conquer Florida but were shipwrecked on the Florida coast. Within months, all but sixty died; by spring 1529, fifteen were left, and soon just four. They survived because they were enslaved by the local Indians and were traded from tribe to tribe, based on their skills as faith healers. After eight years of this, they escaped to Mexico. De Vaca's description of what he saw (*Adventures in the Unknown Interior of America*) is a key source for anthropologists – of which I am one – and it is among other things testimony to how thoroughly established slavery was in the New World long before any possible influence of European interlopers.

The year 1492 changed the world, but not by introducing slavery to the Americas. Slavery was already here. The Spanish initially embraced the idea of enslaving native people, but then thought better of it. First, the

Laws of Burgos, adopted in 1512, attempted to restrain the Spanish abuse of indigenous people. But in 1542, with the issuing of the New Laws of the Indies for the Good Treatment and Preservation of the Indians, the Spanish liberated the Native Americans from this yoke:

> *We ordain and command that from henceforward for no cause of war nor any other whatsoever, though it be under title of rebellion, nor by ransom nor in other manner can an Indian be made a slave, and we will that they be treated as our vassals of the Crown of Castile since such they are.*[2]

The exact meaning of this is debated by historians. It seems the Spanish crown wanted to roll back the encomienda, a form of servitude slightly different from the plantation slavery we are more familiar with. The encomienda gave Spanish holders of land-grants the right to demand tribute and forced labor from the local inhabitants.

By the time the Spanish imposed the New Laws, both the Spanish and the Portuguese had already introduced another form of slavery by forcing captured Africans to labor in New World mines and plantations. By the Treaty of Tordesillas (1494), the Portuguese held the monopoly on bringing slaves from West Africa, but the Spanish provided a ready market. Some of the African slaves were sent to Spanish settlements along what is now the Eastern Seaboard of the United States. In 1526, Lucas Vázquez de Ayllón established a settlement on the coast of Georgia, San Miguel de Gualdape, supplied by African slaves. Enslaved African men were frequently assigned to oversee native American slaves in mines and workshops, for example – and were infamous for the brutality with which they treated them.

The story of African slaves in the Americas during the sixteenth century deserves to be better known, but this is not the place to tell that story. Rather, this book is concerned with the slavery that was indigenous to the New World before Columbus and the introduction of African slavery in the New World by the Spanish and the Portuguese: it is these historical facts that stand in the way of the thesis enunciated in *The New York Times Magazine*'s special issue of August 18, 2019. Bearing a black-and-white photograph of empty ocean, the cover boldly declared:

> *In August of 1619, a ship appeared on this horizon, near Point Comfort, a coastal port in the British colony of Virginia. It carried more than 20 enslaved Africans, who were sold to the colonists. America was not yet America, but this was the moment it began. No aspect of the country that would be formed here has been untouched by the 250 years of slavery that followed. On the 400th anniversary of this fateful moment, it is finally time to tell our story truthfully.*

Inside the magazine, further text explained that the arrival of these slaves "inaugurated a barbaric system of chattel slavery that would last for the next 250 years. This is sometimes referred to as the country's original sin, but it is more than that: It is the country's very origin."[3]

These statements and others like them convey the impression that slavery, or at least African slavery, began in Virginia in 1619. This is false in several ways. Slavery was common practice in Africa and in many other parts of the world long before 1619. Slavery was already in North and South America. Slavery continued among American tribes beyond the reach of Western law well into the nineteenth century.[4] African slavery in particular was common in much of the New World, including the Caribbean, Mexico, and the Spanish territories of what would eventually become the United States. And, it turns out, the status as slaves of those Africans who were sold in Virginia in 1619 is in doubt. More on this later.

The *Times* sets out "to tell our story truthfully," but it does so under a false flag. The truth that can be mined from this is that the slaves who landed in Virginia were the first we know of who were brought *to an English colony on the North American mainland*. That indeed is something, but is it the country's "very origin"?

The answer given by many historians who have responded to the 1619 Project is *no, definitely not*. This book summarizes the historians' arguments, but it goes beyond that to consider some broader questions raised by the 1619 Project. The project itself is a major undertaking by America's most important newspaper. The *Times* invested heavily in the initial publication and in subsequent months followed it up by treating the project as its signature theme. Newspapers do not ordinarily project themselves into a total rewriting of a nation's history, but that is what the *Times* says it is doing. The later, online version declares:

> *The goal of The 1619 Project is to reframe American history by considering what it would mean to regard 1619 as our nation's birth year. Doing so requires us to place the consequences of slavery and the contributions of black Americans at the very center of the story we tell ourselves about who we are as a country.*

Why did the *New York Times* decide to "reframe American history"? Why now? Why this particular frame?

October 1492

Of course, if the *Times* had chosen a quixotic project such as elevating field hockey to be the national pastime, or pushing to make chestnuts the nation's favorite snack food, most of us would have scratched our heads and then shrugged. "Reframing American history" may be just as quixotic, but naturally it strikes us as more serious and consequential – especially when we learn on the last page of that special issue that the *Times* had partnered with the Pulitzer Center to roll out a free 1619 curriculum to schools across the country.

The 1619 Project is not just a journalistic undertaking. It is also an effort to reshape everything that American schoolchildren learn about their country.

This leads to still deeper questions. Why does the study of history matter? Does the study of American history in particular bear special attention? Why does history itself – not just the study of it – matter? The *Times* obviously thinks it does.

Some critics of the 1619 Project believe that it is part of a larger effort to destroy America. That's a stark way to put it, but if America is founded on some core beliefs and the 1619 Projects aims to uproot those beliefs, it might be a necessary question: Is the 1619 Project, in fact, ultimately aimed at destroying America? If so, how exactly does it contribute to such an aim?

To answer those questions, we have to take a step back and ask, What is the *Times'* purpose in launching the 1619 Project? To repeat, why does the *Times* judge that it is time to "reframe" American history?

If the project succeeds in making slavery the distinguishing aspect of American history, what are the likely consequences for the nation? What are the practical effects of advocacy for the 1619 Project?

The 1619 Project aims to change the way American

Preface

schools teach American history in general and slavery in particular. How do our schools currently cover this material? How will the 1619 Project change that?

How many school districts and schools have adopted the 1619 curriculum? What exactly does it mean to adopt it? By what process is it adopted?

On whose intellectual authority did the *Times* make the audacious claims that are the substance of the 1619 Project? So far, I've glanced only at the *Times'* basic idea that American slavery started in Virginia in 1619, but its claims go far beyond that, including rejecting the idea that Patriots waged the Revolutionary War to defend the ideals stated in the Declaration of Independence. Some of the *Times'* 1619 Project assertions run counter to almost everything American historians generally uphold, but the *Times* failed to identify the historians it consulted. So who are the historians behind the 1619 Project?

What should a citizen know about American history? And why is it necessary to know whatever it is one should know?

If we want to stop the 1619 Project, how do we bring it to a halt?

I'm an anthropologist, not a historian, and slavery has not been at the center of my studies. But anthropology provides a powerful lens for examining both cultural continuity and change. My work has focused on how these forces play out in American society over long periods, and it has provided an ample foundation for critiquing the 1619 Project. I have also spent the last ten years as president of the National Association of Scholars (NAS), which has given me a deeper perspective on how elite institutions such as the *New York Times* launch and promote novel ideas, some of which have faint connection to the facts.

NAS's mission is to "uphold the standards of a liberal arts education that fosters intellectual freedom, searches for the truth, and promotes virtuous citizenship." Sometimes that requires taking issue with seemingly authoritative bodies that argue that America is a white supremacist state. Telling the difference between seeming authority and real authority is what legitimate scholars do.

But the 1619 Project came from somewhere, and I suspect it came mostly out of our universities, in which radical identitarian politics and theories of racial oppression have long been taking shape. The way American history is taught in colleges and universities has some bearing on how the *Times* now believes American history should be taught in grade schools and high schools across the country. The liberal arts tradition gives warrant to those who wish to explore the idea that American history should be "reframed" along racialist lines, but it doesn't give warrant to shutting down critics of the 1619 Project or ignoring what they say. Ostracism of dissenting opinions appears to be part of how proponents of the 1619 Project are going about their efforts to install it in the nation's curriculum. Anyone who values intellectual freedom and the search for the truth must cry foul at that kind of evasion. And since NAS promotes "virtuous citizenship," we see ourselves as having some stake in what it means to have a free republic under the rule of law.

This book, however, is *my* statement on the 1619 Project, not the collective view of the National Association of Scholars. I emphasize that because the NAS is playing an active role as a critic of the 1619 Project, and, wherever it seems helpful, I am drawing on the work of my NAS colleagues.

The book starts with my account of the arrival of the Pilgrims in Massachusetts in November 1620, which is to

Preface

say that I endorse a very old idea of the best place to catch the first glimmer of the American republic: 1620, not 1619. I'm well aware that the claims of 1620 have their own weaknesses. The country's "very origin," as the *Times* puts it, isn't something that can be settled once and for all. Many threads from many origins all eventually cohere into a nation. But there is something vital about 1620 that is worth pointing out and that is increasingly lost to national consciousness in our multicultural age. I take nothing away from 1776, 1787, Lincoln's Second Inaugural, or other moments in our history that we think of as foundational. But 1620 is a strong counterpoint to 1619, not just in proximity but in spirit. The rest of the book is best thought of as a voyage of discovery, so I will forgo the usual practice of offering an advance tour of the chapters. What will come, will come.

When we set out to explore a new territory, we hope to have gauged the distance in the right units of measure. But even if we err, we are sometimes saved by a happy accident. I trust this book will have more of Columbus's fortune than that of the Mars Climate Orbiter when it reaches its destination.

CHAPTER ONE

NOVEMBER 1620

Edward Doty signed it. So did Edward Leister.
Both were in their early twenties and were servants
to Stephen Hopkins, a tavern keeper, who signed it as
well. What they signed, along with thirty-eight others,
was an improvised agreement on how they would conduct themselves once they got on shore. That agreement
came to be known as the Mayflower Compact, and it was
signed aboard ship, November 11, 1620.

The two-hundred-word document wasn't drafted
with posterity in mind. It was probably written by William Brewster and William Bradford, two so-called religious Separatists (later called "Pilgrims"), in response to
a practical crisis. Their ship, the *Mayflower*, was supposed
to have brought the would-be settlers to Virginia, where
they would have been under English law and English
protection, but was blown off-course to the shore of what
is now Massachusetts. In that wilderness, the passengers
faced the hardship of a harsh New England winter, the
prospect of lawlessness among themselves, and an
unknown reception from the native inhabitants.

The threat of anarchy was real. Only a minority of those
aboard the *Mayflower* were religious pilgrims – 37 of the 102.

Chapter One

The nonreligious passengers (the Separatists called them "Strangers") quickly asserted that the charter they had signed back in England was void. And some of the Strangers, such as Stephen Hopkins, were rough customers.

Hopkins had been to the New World before. He survived a hurricane shipwreck near Bermuda, only to be convicted of mutiny at Jamestown in 1610 and sentenced to death. His sentence commuted, he returned to England, where he ran an alehouse. Ten years later he was recruited for the *Mayflower* voyage by the London Merchant Adventurers. Hopkins was not someone who was at ease with authority. His servant Edward Doty was even less so. Hot-tempered and quarrelsome, he had a shipboard reputation as a troublemaker.

Other passengers who signed the Mayflower Compact were even younger than Doty and his fellow servant, Leister. George Soule and three others were under twenty-one – an indication that Brewster and Bradford were more concerned with gaining control over a volatile situation than with statesmanship.

By penning the Compact, however, they planted a seed. The document sketched, for the first time in European settlement of the New World, an ideal of self-government based on justice. And it is very important that the leaders invited servants and underage men to sign it as well. The Mayflower Compact was egalitarian in that sense. It ignored class, wealth, and other marks of status – though it did not include women.

The language of the Compact is far less gripping than that of the Declaration of Independence, which would flow primarily from Thomas Jefferson's pen 156 years later. But if you take it in slowly and read it over a few times, it reveals a depth of feeling as well as sturdy practicality:

November 1620

In the name of God, Amen. We, whose names are under-written, the Loyal Subjects of our dread Sovereign Lord King James, by the Grace of God, of Great Britain, France, and Ireland, King, defender of the Faith, etc.:

Having undertaken, for the Glory of God, and advance-ments of the Christian faith, and the honor of our King and Country, a voyage to plant the first colony in the Northern parts of Virginia; do by these presents, solemnly and mutu-ally, in the presence of God, and one another; covenant and combine ourselves together into a civil body politic; for our better ordering, and preservation and furtherance of the ends aforesaid; and by virtue hereof to enact, constitute, and frame, such just and equal laws, ordinances, acts, constitu-tions, and offices, from time to time, as shall be thought most meet and convenient for the general good of the colony; unto which we promise all due submission and obedience.

"These presents" are the forty-one signers, and they "covenant" themselves – in the language of the Old Testa-ment, which permeates the Compact, that is to make the most unbreakable promise of all. They covenant and *combine* themselves, which is to say that the religious Sepa-ratists and the merely adventurous Strangers put aside their profound differences to form a single, and single-minded, group. And not just any group but "a civil body politic."

That's a phrase that these days we are unlikely to encounter outside a textbook. What is "a civil body poli-tic"? It isn't a political party, eager to impose its opinions on those who disagree. It isn't a nation or a state, setting out to govern a people. A "civil body politic" is simply a group of people who agree to govern themselves by common rules to be created through peaceful delibera-tion. That means it isn't a tribe, a dictatorship, or an aristocracy. It offers an ordered public life under the rule of law.

The signers spell that out. Their "civil body politic" is for the "better ordering and preservation" of the community. Better than what? Better than every man for himself. Better than a *Lord of the Flies* vision of what happens to castaways who have committed to no agreement. And "preservation" is serious business. Some of the passengers on the *Mayflower* had already died, and 45 of the original 102 would die of scurvy, exposure, and other ailments before the winter of 1620–1621 was over, in what William Bradford called "the general calamity." Preservation also meant warding off possible attacks by the Indians, who all through the winter kept watch on the Englishmen from a distance, and who "would show themselves aloof" but run away if approached.

The passengers and crew on the *Mayflower* had survived a difficult Atlantic crossing aboard a cargo ship that usually ferried wine and cloth and sometimes herring on the North Sea, occasionally venturing into the Atlantic for trips to Spain. The *Mayflower* had set out from a port on the River Thames in mid-July, all of its passengers recruits of the London Merchant Adventurers, their family members, and servants. It rendezvoused with another ship, the *Speedwell*, which came from Holland with the thirty-seven English Separatists. After meeting, they started out again, but 200 miles west of England, the *Speedwell* sprang a leak. Both ships returned to England, where the *Speedwell* passengers crammed into the *Mayflower*, which finally got underway on September 6. William Bradford believed that the master of the *Speedwell*, to avoid the crossing, had sabotaged his own ship. In any case, the long delay meant that the *Mayflower* was crossing the Atlantic during the stormy season and that it was destined to arrive in North America at the onset of winter.

The *Mayflower* leaked too. In the dire discomfort of the ship's hold, people quarreled and sometimes cheated one another. The Mayflower Compact anticipated that maintaining good order among starving, ill-clothed, sick, and irate people would require a lot more than godly exhortations. It would require efforts to "enact, constitute, and frame, such just and equal laws, ordinances, acts, constitutions, and offices . . . as shall be thought most meet and convenient for the general good of the colony."

"Meet" means appropriate. "Convenient" means timely in light of the crises ahead. A good law that addresses the winter crisis the next summer is not convenient.

How would the little colony go about enacting, constituting, and framing? The Mayflower Compact didn't say. In fact, the group appointed itself a governor and drew on the military skill of its one soldier, Myles Standish. Brewster, Standish, and Bradford earned what authority they had by tireless service fetching wood and making fires, preparing food for the sick, washing infected clothes, and doing so "willingly and cheerfully."

Thus they gained the trust of the survivors, who had promised "all due submission and obedience" to the "just and equal laws" that the Mayflower Compact said would govern the settlement.

The Mayflower Compact has a secure place in American history as one of the first two attempts to conceive a form of self-government on our shores. The other was the formation of the House of Burgesses in Virginia. But neither can really be read as the American founding. The far better claim to being that milestone is the Declaration of Independence, which in 1776 asserted a complete separation of the colonies from the British throne. The Mayflower Compact opens with a reassurance of the opposite:

Chapter One

"We, whose names are underwritten, the Loyal Subjects of our dread Sovereign Lord King James ..." (The House of Burgesses, which I deal with later, was created by a private company.)

The British king, though he was far off and completely unaware of the plight of the *Mayflower* mariners, is evoked as a reminder that the people aboard the ship will sooner or later be accountable for their actions under British law. Reminding the more rambunctious among the crew and passengers that they are "Loyal Subjects" is a way of nudging them not to take too much advantage of their remoteness from controlling institutions of the state.

The Mayflower Compact begins with a terse prayer: "In the name of God, Amen." The Declaration of Independence, by contrast, opens with a self-descriptive label: "The unanimous Declaration of the thirteen united States of America," and immediately moves into august explanation: "When in the Course of human events, it becomes necessary for one people to dissolve the political bands which have connected them with another ..." Further along in that opening sentence, Jefferson mentions "the Laws of Nature and of Nature's God"; but this is no prayer. God is not mentioned again or alluded to until the final sentence of the Declaration: "And for the support of this Declaration, with a firm reliance on the protection of divine Providence, we mutually pledge to each other our Lives, our Fortunes and our sacred Honor."

The Mayflower Compact differs from the Declaration of Independence in numerous ways, but the Compact's initial invocation of God and assertion of loyalty to the king frame it as a call to order. The Declaration is several things: an explanation, a statement of principles, a list of complaints, and a bold assertion of new authority, of a new sovereignty. It grew out of the deliberations of educated men who had the time to debate alternatives.

The Mayflower Compact, by contrast, is a bare statement of purpose coupled with a pledge to join together. The bare purpose is to "plant the first colony in the Northern parts of Virginia" – by which they meant the wilderness where they landed, what became known as Massachusetts. The pledge to join together is entirely a matter for the voyagers themselves. The Declaration addresses itself to the king of England and to the "opinions of mankind," though it implicitly speaks to the American people and the thirteen states as well. The Mayflower Compact imagines no such grand or even external audience. It is written simply for the people who signed it, their families, and the rest of the crew and passengers. Any who chose not to sign would be on notice that they would face a unified opposition should they try to go their own way.

But for all these differences between the Mayflower Compact and the Declaration of Independence, the two are profoundly connected. As Rebecca Fraser put it in her popular history, *The Mayflower: The Families, the Voyage, and the Founding of America*, "the Mayflower Compact has a whisper of the contractual government enunciated in the 4 July 1776 Declaration of Independence, that governments derive their just powers 'from the consent of the governed.'"[1]

Both documents are attempts to forge a new unity – "a civil body politic" – out of disparate people who have conflicting interests. Both call into existence a new government, and both justify that government as needed for safety, good order, and justice. Above all, both project the ideal of self-government as the only way to achieve the "general good."

The circumstances differ so greatly between 1620 and

1776 that it is easy to lose sight of these connections. But the connections are real, not coincidental. The Separatists – that is, Englishmen separated from the Church of England – in 1620 were the first Europeans in the New World who imagined for themselves a self-governing community independent (at least for the time being) of the society from which they had emigrated. Circumstances, however, required something more than a self-enclosed community of fellow dissenters from the Church of England. They had to imagine a form of government that would also justly govern men such as Edward Doty, Edward Leister, Stephen Hopkins, and the other Strangers.

The government that these Puritan pioneers formed was by no means liberal. The British Crown eventually (in 1692) had to force the Massachusetts Bay Colony to tolerate members of other sects. The colony did not welcome Quakers, and dissenters had to pay a fee to support the Puritan church. But these were later developments. The Mayflower Pilgrims in 1620 and the years following were concerned with building a viable community, where survival itself was a question, and where the help of the Strangers was crucial. They believed divine Providence had brought them to Massachusetts, but it was a hard Providence that required them to loot grain stored in abandoned Indian villages and take other actions that hardly seem worthy of people on a religious quest.

The Mayflower Compact dealt not with membership in a church. Rather it announced the creation of a community that included all sorts, Separatists and Strangers alike. The actual community that resulted became a model for New England villages and towns and ultimately for the nation. It was a literate community that emphasized education. In time New England teachers would carry this model west, and it would become a foundational idea of who we are as a people. It was, of course, not the only model that Americans would look to. The colonies and later the states of the American South would offer competing ideals of self-government and develop a system of county identity. But the New England model proved the stronger of the two.

The Compact was not the actual American founding, but a crucial pre-founding, informing the beginning of the American republic. It was a rough-and-tumble beginning, with death by starvation and disease awaiting many. But it has rightly been seen as the moment when an idea of true self-government began to take root.

CHAPTER TWO

AUGUST 1619

E DWARD DOTY and Edward Leister were among several English servants who landed at Plymouth in
November. The *Mayflower* brought no slaves to the new
colony. Fifteen months earlier, however, English pirates
had landed some twenty to thirty African captives at
Jamestown, Virginia. The exact status of these captives is
unclear. It is likely that they were considered slaves on
board the pirate ship, but because slavery was not recognized by English common law, once the captives landed
their status became fuzzy. In Bermuda, also founded by
the Virginia Company, slaves brought by outsiders were
considered to be indentures with a life tenure of service.
In Virginia, the records show that many of the captives
were, after a term of indenture, set free. None were
recorded as slaves.

Because the *New York Times* in its 1619 Project has
declared that the arrival of these captives "inaugurated a
barbaric system of chattel slavery that would last the next
250 years," the event deserves careful scrutiny. The *Times*
argues that the captives were sold as slaves and that the
event is best understood as the true founding of America.
"America was not yet America, but this was the moment
it began."

The situation, however, is murkier than that. The primary source for what happened in August 1619 is a report from a Virginia settler, John Rolfe, who in January 1620 told the Virginia Company treasurer:

> *About the latter end of August, a Dutch man of Warr of the burden of a 160 tunnes arrived at Point-Comfort, the Commandors name Capt Jope, his pilott for the West Indies one Mr Marmaduke an Englishman. They mett wth the Trier [the ship Treasurer] in the West Indyes, and determyned to hold consort shipp hetherward, but in their passage lost one the other. He brought not any thing but 20. and odd Negroes, wch the Governor [Sir George Yeardley] and Cape Merchant [Abraham Peirsey] bought for victualle (whereof he was in greate need as he pretended) at the best and easyest rate they could.*[1]

Rolfe was a figure to be reckoned with. He is also remembered for his marriage in 1614 to Pocahontas and for his introduction to Virginia of a Trinidadian variety of sweet tobacco that proved to be the colony's first successful export.

Trading food to Captain Jope for captive people certainly *sounds* like slavery, but the colony at the time had no system of slavery as such. When the records of this time refer to "slaves," they generally mean Englishmen who had been convicted of crimes and who were punished by a period of involuntary servitude. In May 1618, for example, the deputy-governor of the Virginia colony proclaimed that residents who failed to attend compulsory church services would "be a slave the following week."[2] Human labor could not be wasted by imprisoning those who broke the law.

So what happened to the "20 and odd Negroes" that

Captain Jope brought to Jamestown? It is a matter of debate. Many historians have long held that they were assimilated to the status of indentured laborers, which was the colony's primary source of human labor. Under that system, they would have earned their freedom after a period of years doing mainly agricultural work. Not every form of forced labor is "slavery" in the sense we commonly think. The status of these African captives appears to have fallen into a vaguely defined middle ground. Unlike English indentured servants, they had not signed up for an excursion to Virginia. But unlike the slaves of later times, they had a genuine opportunity to work their way out of bondage, and they had basic rights under the law. A major scholarly examination of the African Americans at Jamestown, published in 2003, suggests that the best term for the condition of the involuntary immigrants of 1619 is "servitude," and that the transition to slavery lay years into the future.[3]

Not all historians agree. Most notably, Alden T. Vaughan, writing in the 1980s, concluded that all the Negroes who were brought to Virginia in this early period were considered slaves, not indentured servants.[4]

Tim Hashaw, who styles himself an "investigative journalist," is even more insistent that the captives were enslaved. Hashaw's 2007 book, *The Birth of Black America: The First African Americans and the Pursuit of Freedom at Jamestown*, has become the go-to source for those who endorse the *Times'* 1619 narrative. But it is an odd book, in the form of an elaborate conspiracy theory indicting as a liar John Rolfe, the one named witness we have to the arrival of Captain Jope's ship that year. Hashaw believes he has uncovered "a secret Puritan conspiracy at the highest levels of seventeenth-century Europe."[5] It is an entertaining story that, like any good conspiracy theory, weaves together an abundance of well-established facts with threads of sheer invention. We do now know quite a bit about the circumstances that led to the arrival of that ship in Jamestown, but it requires some leaps of imagination to reach Hashaw's conclusion that Rolfe was helping to run a clandestine pirate base out of Jamestown as part of a transatlantic operation by Puritans to undermine King James I.

More likely what we have in the arrival of that pirate ship is just another instance of the clumsy opportunism of high-seas brigands. The fuller story of what happened, however, does deserve attention.[6] A few days or weeks after Captain Jope's arrival at Jamestown on his ship the *White Lion*, a second pirate ship, the *Treasurer*, arrived and landed about six more African captives. The *White Lion* and the *Treasurer* had together intercepted the Spanish slave ship *San Juan Bautista*, which was headed to the port of Veracruz, Mexico. The pirates between them appropriated about sixty of the captives. The *Treasurer* apparently sold some of these captives in Bermuda before heading northwest to Jamestown.

A census of Jamestown taken in March 1620 reported fifteen African men and seventeen African women, presumably all the survivors of the *San Juan Bautista*'s original cargo of 350 captives. These thirty-two individuals had suffered terrible hardships, but they were fortunate in one respect. Had the *San Juan Bautista* arrived in Veracruz, its human cargo would have been sold to labor in the Mexican silver mines – and almost certain early death. Jamestown offered them an opportunity to live and even to thrive. The oppression they were to bear as involuntary captives in the British colony was the less onerous yoke compared to what they had already been through and what other African captives faced under Spanish rule.

How much less onerous is evident in the subsequent

careers of some of those who endured servitude along the shores of the Chesapeake. An especially well-attested case was an individual known as Antonio, who may have been among those individuals sold by Captain Jope in 1619, though he doesn't enter the historical record until two years later when he was set to work on the Bennett family plantation.[7] He was eventually freed, renamed himself Anthony Johnson, got married, raised children, became a plantation owner himself, and acquired African slaves of his own. He successfully sued one of his white neighbors in a Virginia court.[8] Plainly, Virginian "slavery" was not a total institution then, nor would it ever become so in the antebellum South.

DO THE FACTS MATTER?

The *Times'* 1619 Project commences with a historical claim that doesn't match the known facts. Jake Silverstein writes that the arrival of those "20 to 30 enslaved Africans" in Virginia "inaugurated a barbaric system of chattel slavery that would last for the next 250 years."[9]

A social system based on chattel slavery that was frequently barbaric did eventually arise in some of the British North American colonies, but in Virginia it did not arise until more than half a century later, and even then in small steps. The *New York Times'* sloppiness about historical facts is one reason to approach with caution its claims about 1619 as the decisive moment in America's descent into racial despotism. But it is hardly the only reason. The *Times* sets alarm bells ringing because *they don't seem to care whether their facts are correct.*

The *Times'* attitude can fairly be summarized thus: *What difference does the year make? Slavery commenced at some point during the English colonization of the Atlantic seaboard – if not in*

August 1619

1619, then a little later. The year 1619 is a convenient date because it was exactly four hundred years before the New York Times *proclaimed it as the origin, and because it is well-established as the point when captive Africans were introduced to Jamestown.* In other words, even if the *Times* is mistaken on what actually happened, for the paper's editors the symbolic value of the story outweighs any concerns about its factual accuracy.

Both the *Times,* and those who brush aside its factual sloppiness from sympathy with its larger aims, open themselves to self-deception. The *Times'* willingness to embrace fake-but-accurate history means they are all too likely to embrace history that is both fake and inaccurate – and not even realize how far they have strayed from the true record of the past.

Moreover, when the editors responsible for the 1619 Project have been confronted with the errors and contradictions of the *Times'* portrayal of history, they have retreated into a postmodern claim that it is all a *matter of interpretation.* This is exactly what Silverstein, the *Times* magazine's editor in chief, wrote in response to five major historians whose letter to the magazine was published on December 29, 2019. The letter expressed the historians' "strong reservations about important aspects of The 1619 Project." The letter, by Victoria Bynum, James M. McPherson, James Oakes, Sean Wilentz, and Gordon S. Wood – five of America's most prominent academic historians – is important in its own right, and I will come back to it later in this book. But Silverstein's response is jaw-dropping. Refusing to correct any of the inaccuracies, he explains:

> *Historical understanding is not fixed; it is constantly being adjusted by new scholarship and new voices. Within the*

world of academic history, differing views exist, if not over what precisely happened, then about why it happened, who made it happen, how to interpret the motivations of historical actors and what it all means.[10]

Historical understanding indeed changes as new facts are brought to light and contexts are better established, but that is never a license to ignore facts that are already established. Silverstein's defense that "historical understanding is not fixed" is a sleight of hand, because the five historians challenged the *Times* about its errors concerning well-known, uncontroverted facts. Silverstein, however, used this specious rationale as warrant to bask in the complacent comfort that the *Times* has accomplished "what we hoped our project would do: expand the reader's sense of the American past." He is blind to the difference between expanding the reader's sense by presenting real history and expanding it into the realm of pseudohistorical polemic.

Silverstein's gambit, alas, is likely to fool most readers. Americans may have become familiar with the dangers of "fake news," but fake history is more insidious. Fake news is typically met with rebuttals by many people who know the facts. Fake history, by contrast, often settles into the background as something "everybody knows." Professional historians and others who have a keen interest in a topic will raise protests, but these can seem like pebbles of fact tossed against an ocean of falsehood. The 1619 mythology in particular will reach millions of Americans who never read the original *Times* declarations of August 2019 and never heard of the 1619 Project itself, but who have been exposed to hundreds of the reverberations – the waves in that ocean of falsehood – that wash over popular culture.

August 1619

I should also note that some critics of the 1619 Project have been willing to shrug at the *Times'* 1619 origin myth. For these critics, the more urgent need is to combat the racial rancor and emphasis on victimhood that pervade the 1619 mythology, and to reestablish the Declaration of Independence as the founding moment of the American republic. They point out that scholarly disputes about what happened in coastal Virginia four hundred years ago are unlikely to move the many millions of Americans whose interest is aroused by the prospect of a new way of looking at our history through the lens of racial oppression.

That's only partly correct. Historical facts still matter to many thousands, and the thousands we can persuade about the facts now will help persuade the millions later. The facts may only be pebbles, but amassing them can make a breakwater to bar the tempest of deceit. So I will take some trouble in these pages to join those professional historians who bear witness to the truth, and summarize what actually happened in Virginia in the early seventeenth century.

Let's look a little deeper at the point of origin.

SLAVERIES

We twenty-first-century Americans have certain ideas about what slavery was and what it is. The auction block, the whipping post, and the plantation slave quarters come instantly to mind. Images in popular culture alternately picture slavery in the antebellum South as a kind of cross-racial family bond, as in Margaret Mitchell's *Gone with the Wind* (1936) and the Hollywood movie version of it (1939), and as a horrific experience, as in Toni Morrison's *Beloved* (1987). Modern views come down decisively in favor of the horrific, which is in keeping with Harriet Beecher Stowe's abolitionist novel *Uncle Tom's Cabin* (1852). But before the advent of modernity, all the world's great religions, without exception, had given slavery authoritative approval.

What we know of slavery is that it was a system in which members of one race were denied most (but not all) legal rights and were treated as the personal property of their owners. The legal rights of slaves varied over time and from place to place, but masters did not have unlimited power over slaves, at least in the eyes of the law. Slave owners could and did violate those laws. Corporal punishments and separating husbands and wives and selling their children were common. The barbarity of the system was both physical and psychological.

Research on the history of slavery has complicated this picture. We now know that many slaves succeeded in keeping their marriages and their children together. We know that some slaves became skilled artisans who were able to accumulate wealth and sometimes purchase their own freedom. We know that most masters took care of the health of their slaves if for no other reason than the need to protect valuable property. We know that thousands of free persons of color owned slaves. But these qualifications convince no one that slavery was a positive good, as was once argued by figures such as John C. Calhoun.

The contemporary practice of human trafficking for prostitution also contributes strongly to our understanding of antebellum slavery. Campaigns against it claim that up to fifty thousand people a year are trafficked, more than half children, and the majority from Mexico and the Philippines. Estimates of the number of people worldwide caught up in this kind of slavery range from twenty million to forty million.[11] This is worth keeping in mind as an example of how the term "slavery" can be extended to widely divergent forms of human exploitation. What nineteenth-century Southern chattel slavery and modern human trafficking for sex have in common is the radical denial of one person's individual freedom by another.

The brute fact of such oppression makes it hard to get a clear conceptual picture of what slavery is. We wouldn't ordinarily consider as a form of slavery a religious devotee, such as a cloistered monk or nun, who had voluntarily given up personal freedom. Nor do we think of incarcerated prisoners as slaves, though they may be required to perform labor for nominal pay. A salaried worker who feels unable to leave a job because he needs health-insurance benefits or because he is waiting for his stock options to vest is nobody's slave, though he may feel his personal freedom is radically denied. Where does human autonomy leave off and slavery begin?

In my academic discipline of social anthropology, the concept of slavery gets even more complicated because the purpose of enslaving others has varied among human societies. Coercing people to perform manual labor, such as working in tobacco or cotton fields, was seldom the point in sub-Saharan Africa. In some African societies the defining feature of a slave was that he or she had no rights over his or her children. Elsewhere, slaves were merely a commodity collected for their value in trade for other commodities. In some West African kingdoms such as Benin, slaves provided the fodder for large-scale human sacrifices, and much the same can be said of the Aztecs in Mexico.[12] The Ottoman Turks enslaved Europeans to build their armies. In still other societies, slavery took the form of debt bondage, and a debtor could in principle work his way back to freedom.

This spectrum of possibilities must be kept in mind

because the Southern system of plantation slavery did not spring into existence all at once or fully formed. It evolved over time in different contexts according to a host of variable conditions.

Moreover, in the early and middle years of the seventeenth century in Virginia, the subjection of Africans to bondage labor appears not to have resulted initially in any permanent legal disabilities. We know, for example, that men and women released from bondage acquired considerable property and married, often to white settlers. Ira Berlin recounts that "at least one man from every leading free black family – the Johnsons, Paynes, and Drigguses – married a white woman." And "free black women joined together with white men. William Greensted, a white attorney who represented Elizabeth Key, a woman of color, in her successful suit for freedom, later married her." Berlin depicts a world, especially prior to 1640, in which black and white laborers could "take shelter in the same laws and customs," and even as race-specific laws began to be enacted, blacks and whites mingled freely, drinking, gambling, and celebrating together.[13]

This picture cannot be reconciled with the image of race-based chattel slavery. It seems especially important that the masters in this period had limited rights over the time of their "slaves" and over their bodies. The summer workweek was five and a half days, with holidays off; and "when planters wished to discipline workers, whether black or white, they often used the courts; not until the next century did slave owners presume that they were absolute sovereigns within the confines of their estate."[14] Even then, slave owners faced constraints. Throughout the South in the antebellum period, states moved to qualify the power of individual masters – a movement led by masters themselves to rein in the worst among themselves.

Berlin's account is disputed by some other authorities, notably James Horn in *1619: Jamestown and the Forging of American Democracy*. Horn supplies further details gleaned from the records about the individuals and then turns to the key question: "Did slavery and racial prejudice gradually evolve in Virginia during the half century following the arrival of the Angolans, or did de facto enslavement of Africans begin in 1619?" Horn weighs the evidence carefully, noting the "absence of legislation formally legalizing slavery in early Virginia," but ultimately concludes that "the condition of Africans, including the first Angolans, was undoubtedly slavery."[15]

"Undoubtedly" is often what we say when doubt hangs heavily over a topic and no clear answer is at hand. If what the captives of the *White Lion* endured in Virginia is rightly called slavery, it was a far more fluid and flexible form of slavery, a form of bondage before slave codes came into existence. That is not a distinction that matters to Nikole Hannah-Jones, the architect of the *Times*' 1619 Project. She writes simply, "Those men and women who came ashore on that August day were the beginning of American slavery. They were among the 12.5 million Africans who would be kidnapped from their homes and brought in chains across the Atlantic Ocean in the largest forced migration in human history until the Second World War."[16]

This is expressed in bold indignation, but it collapses history into myth. Untold millions of Africans had been trafficked by Arabs and others for perhaps a thousand years before the Atlantic slave trade began. While a heartbreaking 12.5 million Africans were transported across the Atlantic, the number shipped to North America was only 388,000.[17] Hannah-Jones fires her indignation at British North America, but she loads her weapon with numbers from Mexico, the Caribbean, and Brazil. The vast majority of the slaves that were later brought to the English colonies on coastal America were purchased (not kidnapped) from the West African slave-trading kingdoms. The slaves taken by the Portuguese for transport to Brazil and Spanish America were largely from West-Central Africa, the kingdoms of Kongo and Ndongo, for example, and had been captured in internal wars. Catholicism had become the state religion of the kingdom of Kongo by the end of the fifteenth century. Thus, some of those enslaved in Africa were at least nominal Christians.

From this distance those distinctions may seem not to matter much, but in fact they point to a history rather different from the one Hannah-Jones conjures. Those men and women who were enslaved were not the "beginning of American slavery" but people who, against all odds, had survived an ordeal. In at least some cases they emerged from servitude to become landowners and independent farmers, and created entirely new lives for themselves. America was not yet a place with a fixed identity or even founding ideals. It was sheer possibility. And in some sense these captives recognized it.

We can all wish that these fluid possibilities would have eventually produced a society not stratified by master and slave and racial oppression. But it is a serious misrepresentation of the past to read into the arrival in Jamestown of "20 and odd Negroes" in August 1619 the beginning of slavery and racial oppression in America. Indeed, nowhere on the planet in 1619 can one find an advanced society or civilization functioning without servitude and forms of prejudice and hierarchy.

Was the arrival of the *White Lion* at Jamestown really the founding event of what would become the American republic? No. It was something, but not that – a minor incident that casts light on a small-scale society that as yet had no firm boundaries or abiding sense of purpose.

VIRGINIA

On July 30, 1619, a few weeks before the arrival of the *White Lion*, Virginia's General Assembly convened for the first time. It was a signal event in American history, sometimes described as "the beginning of self-government" in British North America.[18] Under instructions from the Virginia Company, Sir George Yeardly, whom the company had appointed governor of the colony, called a representative government to order. The General Assembly was to consist of himself as governor, a Council of State appointed by the company, and twenty-two elected representatives of constituencies that Yeardly designated. These representatives came two each from various settlements (James City, Charles City, the City of Henricus, etc.) and various plantations (Martin's Hundred, Captain Ward's Plantation, Flowerdew, etc.).

Historians have spent considerable effort figuring out the relationships between the English crown, the privately owned Virginia Company, and the instruments of local government that the Virginia Company created in Virginia under English law. The Virginia enterprise was conceived as a "commonwealth," meant to protect the legal rights of the settlers as well as the company's interests. Before Yeardly was instructed to convene the General Assembly, the colony had been under martial law and "the largely unrestricted powers of the governor."[19]

The creation of Virginia's General Assembly is rightly understood to be a key event in British colonization. It planted a seed of self-government, but it was a seed planted in a different system, far more commercial in character from the outset than was the "commonwealth" created by the Mayflower Compact, in which forty-one individuals "covenanted" and combined themselves into a new "civil body politic."

In Virginia, the General Assembly was imposed by a chartered English corporation. At Plymouth, the settlers invented their own government. In Virginia, the representative body was constructed exclusively of members of the established interests. At Plymouth, care was taken to win the consent even of indentured servants and legal minors. In Virginia, the Virginia Company intended to put in place a system of laws that guaranteed "liberty and reward" and under which every person could know "what he or she may forever challenge as their right." Those words were written by someone initialed "R.F." in a letter conveying some of the company's instructions to Governor Yeardly. R.F. continued:

> *Last they [the laws] set down what lands or immunities every person is presently to enjoy, according to their merit and quality, and what duties they are tied to, besides many other particulars too long here to write. . . .*
>
> *And these laws and ordinances are not to be chested or hidden like a candle under a bushel, but in the form of a Magna Carta to be Published to the whole colony, to the end every particular person though never so mean, may both for his own right challenge it and in case he be at any time wronged, through by the best of the country, he may have law to allege for his speedy remedy.*[20]

R.F., speaking for the Virginia Company, plainly conveys some distrust of the colony's political elite, whom he suspects will not be eager to convey the news to the common folk that they have enforceable rights under the law. The language also makes clear that the new system is intended to uphold the distinctions of "merit and quality" among the colonists, although it gives some protections to those lower on the social scale who had suffered considerably under the previous system of aristocratic domination.

The situation at Plymouth differed profoundly. Daniel Webster, invited to speak at Plymouth's bicentenary anniversary in 1820, emphasized how the community freed itself from the burden of aristocratic rule, with "no lands yielding rent, and no tenants rendering service." Plymouth pivoted to "political institutions" that respected private property divided equitably. It abolished primogeniture, and property "was all freehold."[21] This was a small-scale egalitarian community that aimed at something more than just self-rule. It aimed at maintaining the freedom and dignity of individuals. Webster no doubt exaggerates. The Plymouth colonists were not immune to self-interest, but they plainly started out in an egalitarian spirit.

When the Angolan slaves set foot on Virginia soil in August 1619, they happened to arrive at exactly the moment when it had been ordained that "every particular person though never so mean" had legal rights and remedies. Whether we call these individuals slaves or captives or indentured servants or (as the records sometimes put it) simply Negroes, they had rights, and it was not long before some of them realized it and took successful action. The Virginia Company had not foreseen the arrival of "slaves" and had made no special provision for them. The General Assembly appeared in no haste to distinguish these involuntary immigrants from other laborers, and so for several decades the colony accommodated itself to people pursuing their interests with little regard to racial distinction. This fluidity, of course, was not to last, but for a time, race in America harbored an alternative future.

CHAPTER THREE

AUGUST 2019

THE SUBSTANCE OF the 1619 Project cannot be separated from its packaging. The project is above all a media campaign, which commenced with the publication of the special issue of *The New York Times Magazine*. Once that is understood, we can see how the project's content falls into place.

Let's start with the cover of that special issue. It features a black-and-white photo of an empty ocean horizon, with these words superimposed on dark water:

In August of 1619, a ship appeared on this horizon, near Point Comfort, a coastal port in the English colony of Virginia. It carried more than 20 enslaved Africans, who were sold to the colonists. No aspect of the country that would be formed here has been untouched by the years of slavery that followed. On the 400th anniversary of this fateful moment, it is finally time to tell our story truthfully.

No ship appears on the horizon: just a calm, featureless sea under a cloudy, gray sky.

Inside the magazine is a note titled "Behind the Cover" that credits Dannielle Bowman with the photo of "the water off the coast of Hampton, Va., at the site where the first enslaved Africans were recorded being brought to Britain's North American colonies." The note also explains that this story is left out of our "national narratives" and "founding myths": "Rarely is the disembarking of these people treated with grandeur. We wanted to change that."

Grandeur seems an odd choice of words for that particular story. In any case, the image is bleak, ominous, foreboding, tinged with the angst of unnatural absence. Grandeur is not its mood. It is an image of barrenness and isolation. When I first saw the cover, I imagined the point was to capture the despair of the slaves looking back at the immensity that cut them off from their past lives. Is the immensity of hopelessness the grandeur that the *Times* intended to evoke?

Whatever the original intention, the *Times* has stuck with that ocean image. In the months following the project's rollout, the newspaper featured full-page advertisements for the 1619 Project that consist of a similar image presented in landscape orientation, with "1619" superimposed on it, with a facing page that displays "2019" on an empty, blue-gray background. The new 1619 seascape includes spits of land and a touch of shore, but the most noticeable difference is the addition of color, which lends a little vivacity to the empty scene. The *Times* was evidently feeling upbeat, as attested by the advertising copy that adorns the pages: "Journalism that confronts our assumptions ... The truth can change how we see the world." Additional text touts how the *Times* "covers the world in all its complexity" and extols the 1619 Project as exploring "how slavery has shaped everything in America, from music to traffic to capitalism – even our democracy itself."

The companion page, 2019, offers similar bromides:

"The truth is worth it . . . and sparks important dialogue." The copy mentions a five-part podcast that is part of the 1619 Project and a curriculum to be "taught in all 50 states." It promises to continue the work "throughout 2020."

These are advertisements, not arguments, but they convey a good deal of the spirit of the 1619 Project. For an endeavor that presents itself as declaring a world-changing truth, the project is marred by an astonishing number of errors, misstatements, and omissions. And for a project that purports to cover the world "in all its complexity," 1619 gives us a just-so story of simplistic generalities – *slavery has shaped everything in America*. Indeed, the promised "dialogue" has consisted mostly of Nikole Hannah-Jones's monologues and conversations with the like-minded. Bowman's cover photo may not have captured "grandeur," but it is a good representation of the 1619 Project's spacious emptiness.

On February 9, 2020, the *Times* amplified the 1619 campaign – now officially part of the paper's "The Truth Is Worth It" campaign begun in 2017 – by launching a fifty-second TV commercial during the Academy Awards. In the commercial, Janelle Monáe, a singer, songwriter, and actress, stands ankle deep in the same surf that appears in the print advertisements. This time, however, the photography is in gleaming color. Monáe is wearing a flowing white robe with a frilled collar. *Adweek* declared that she is "the first celebrity in an advertisement for *The New York Times*."[1]

After the Oscars, the ad was then posted to the internet, where it has been widely viewed. Ms. Monáe recites a slightly condensed and altered version of the original 1619 Project text:

Chapter Three

In August of 1619, a ship appeared on this horizon, near Point Comfort, Virginia. It carried more than 20 enslaved Africans, who were sold to the colonists. No aspect of the country we know today has been untouched by the years of slavery that followed. America was not yet America but this was the moment it began.

The visual technique and the soundtrack of the commercial also deserve note. The ad opens with Monáe in the distance, perhaps a hundred feet away, centered in the landscape. A leafy branch hangs over the scene and beach grass sways in the breeze, as the camera slowly zooms in on Monáe. We hear birds chirping, the lapping of the waves, and a very low, ominous hum from a string ensemble, featuring a double bass and cello. The piece is in E minor, a common choice for portentous cinematic scenes. As Monáe begins to speak, the music becomes more audible, and at the point where she says "No aspect of the country" it crescendos with a plaintively swelling G played by a French horn against the background of strings.

It is classic scary-movie music. Monáe finishes her speech at 27 seconds, and the camera moves past her to the empty ocean. The music continues, but the creaking of wood and scattered voices subtly suggest the arrival of that slave ship echoing down through the centuries.

Monáe first became known as a singer in 2003 and gained wider fame as a vocalist on the hit "We Are Young" (2011). In the video for the song, she appears for a few seconds standing impeccably composed in a tuxedo in the midst of a crashing bar fight: an arresting image. She subsequently starred in the Hollywood movies *Hidden Figures* and *Moonlight*, which was awarded the Oscar for best picture in 2016. With her star power, Monáe does indeed add glamour if not *grandeur* to the *Times'* project.

All of this is to say that the *Times* has spared nothing in its promotional campaign for the 1619 Project. Its advertisements are richly emotional efforts to manipulate audiences into acquiescing to a story that is fundamentally false. Historians publishing articles that detail the numerous inaccuracies in the *Times'* pseudohistory are up against a famous, popular, and distinctive singer-actress and a soundtrack that dictates what your feelings should be. It is no contest.

Advertising is just one piece of the *Times'* promotional campaign for the 1619 Project. Nikole Hannah-Jones, the project's chief architect and the author of the first essay in the special issue of the magazine, has presented herself on Twitter and in public speaking as its leading advocate. Hannah-Jones had already established herself as a significant figure in advocacy journalism well before the 1619 Project. Using the Twitter name "Ida Bae Wells" (a play on Ida B. Wells, a civil-rights crusader-journalist), she describes herself in her Twitter bio as "the Beyoncé of Journalism." What exactly this means is open to interpretation, but it points to her diva-like personality and her (desire for) celebrity.

Hannah-Jones's reputation pre–1619 Project was based on her writings about school segregation. In 2017 the MacArthur Foundation, known for its extravagant financial support for progressive activists (as well as others in the sciences, humanities, and arts), awarded her one of its "genius" grants for "chronicling the persistence of racial segregation in American society, particularly in education, and reshaping national conversations around education reform." An admiring journalist writing in 2017 singled out as her chief accomplishments two major articles about school segregation, "Segregation Now" (2014) and "Choosing a School for My Daughter in a Segregated City," and a two-part radio broadcast for *This American Life*, "The Problem We All Live With" (2015).[2]

In January 2019, Hannah-Jones approached the senior editors of the *New York Times* and proposed the work that became the 1619 Project. This came in the midst of ongoing racial tensions at the *Times*, and the editors quickly agreed to her terms.[3] Hannah-Jones had achieved a position of some authority at the newspaper and was in many respects exempt from ordinary forms of accountability. That becomes evident in what happened after the 1619 Project was launched.

Hannah-Jones has also helped the 1619 Project along by accepting numerous public-speaking invitations. Following the launch of the project in August 2019, numerous historians, other scholars, and journalists began raising questions about the factual accuracy of the essays the *Times* had published as well as the tone and theme of the project. I take up the substance of those critiques in the next chapter. The immediate issue is that Hannah-Jones had been challenged on what might be called matters of journalistic integrity. The speaking invitations gave her an open-ended opportunity to debate with her critics, or short of that, at least to offer refutations of their points. But this is not what happened.

Although faced with criticisms from such eminent historians as Gordon Wood, James McPherson, James Oakes, Richard Carwardine, Clayborne Carson, and Sean Wilentz, Hannah-Jones has found no particular reason to respond to them. Her agent, the Lavin Agency Speakers Bureau, appears to have been extraordinarily successful at booking her exclusively in venues where audiences greet her as a hero, a prophet, or a "genius."[4] Her appearances include a talk at the University of Chicago Institute of Politics, a podcast interview with MSNBC's Chris Hayes, and another with the writer, critic, and former MSNBC cohost Touré.[5]

As of this writing, she has spoken at some forty public events dealing with the 1619 Project. Eighteen of these featured her speaking solo; at the other twenty-two, she shared the stage with one or more speakers – a total of forty-nine of them. Many of these were billed as "dialogues." Given the topic, one might think that historical experts would be among the people most likely to be summoned to "dialogue." But none of the forty-nine interlocutors is a known critic of the 1619 thesis; only three hold a doctoral degree in history, and one more has a master's degree in history. The others come from a variety of fields in which it is easy to imagine they have something to say about racism in America. But it is not so clear that they are prepared to wrestle with a far-reaching revision of American history. Fifteen of the dialoguers were fellow journalists, and four of these were themselves *Times* journalists. Six of the dialoguers came from the field of English composition and literature, though one of these was Henry Louis Gates Jr., who has serious standing in history. Five were lawyers; four came from the arts; three from the discipline of public policy; two each from economics, education, and religion; one each from philosophy, political science, and business. The rest are unidentifiable.

Of course, people from all fields may have important things to say about the 1619 Project. But in their public events, Hannah-Jones and the *Times'* other prominent voices on 1619 have been focused so far on perfecting harmonious agreement with their original ideas. Hannah-Jones has made many appearances, but at none of them has any form of intellectual challenge been welcomed. The word for this is not "dialogue." It is propaganda.

This is, of course, freedom of speech in action. The *Times* and Hannah-Jones are well within their rights to ignore their critics and to create a bubble in which everyone appears to agree with their views. But this approach nullifies any real claim to intellectual seriousness. We seek the truth through pointed examination of the evidence and careful review of the arguments, not through grand pronouncements before worshipful audiences.

At the podium, Hannah-Jones is brusque and confident, especially when delivering opinions that ought to raise questions for any listener. At the University of Chicago, for example, she was asked about how she decided what to include in the 1619 Project. As part of her answer, she told the audience: "The conceit of the magazine, if you haven't read it, is that you can look across almost every aspect of American life whether you think it has to do with slavery or not and with some very rigorous scholarship we were going to show you that it does."[6] It seems noteworthy that she knew in advance that "almost every aspect of American life" has "to do with slavery": this judgment precedes the "rigorous scholarship" she says was undertaken. In other words, she was sure the evidence would be found to underwrite the conclusions she had already reached.

Off the stage, Hannah-Jones conveys a more challenging persona. In a tweet on August 14, 2019, she kicked off the campaign to publicize the 1619 Project with a simple restatement of its purpose:

> *The #1619Project published online today and it is my profound hope that we will reframe for our readers the way we*

understand our nation, the legacy of slavery, and most importantly, the unparalleled role black people have played in this democracy.

But she soon followed with aggressive put-downs of those who challenged her and the project. Most of these tweets have since been deleted, but a few were preserved by critics. In November 2019, for example, she mixed it up with socialists, whom she accused of lying about statements she made:

> *Because here's the thing chief – you give away the game when instead of just critiquing the content of what I say and write, you childishly insult my intellect and then simply make shit up that you know isn't true. It is always a sign of weakness and you are clearly weak.*

The target of this invective replied by posting a recording of Hannah-Jones saying exactly what she denied having said.[7]

In February 2020, after a group of mostly black intellectuals organized by the Woodson Center published their critique (the "1776 Project," later called "1776 Unites") of the 1619 Project, Hannah-Jones tweeted twice. Mark Hemingway of *RealClearPolitics* assesses these emanations:

> *"I want to say this is my response to the 1776 project," she tweeted, followed by a picture of her pointing at her bottom row of gold teeth with her pinky, a dismissive and deeply unserious hip-hop gesture. She followed that up with a "serious" tweet where she suggested that her African-American critics at the 1776 Project didn't actually care about the enslaved children at the time of America's founding. (She later deleted the tweets.)*

Hemingway then delivers the coup de grâce: "In her zeal to escalate every disagreement and answer all criticism with ad hominem attacks, her Twitter persona is very much like . . . Donald Trump's."[8]

Sometimes Hannah-Jones is angry; sometimes she seems deeply confused. Rich Lowry, the editor of *National Review*, took note of a pair of heads-I-win, tails-you-lose tweets on September 6 and 7. Hannah-Jones one day tweets that "America was not exceptional as we're taught. It was just one of many nations for which slavery was foundational to society." The next day she tweets, "But also, how many of these other slave nations were founded on the individual rights of humankind, on the premise that all men were created equal, that they would lead a government of the people, for the people, by the people. THIS is what makes American slavery exceptional."[9] So the United States is not exceptional in any good sense. It is exceptional only in its hypocrisy, because the nation had both slavery *and* ideals that militated against slavery. Of course, Hannah-Jones is wrong here too. Other nations also had both slavery and emancipatory ideals.

Mostly, Hannah-Jones goes in search of hidden racism. In a March 1, 2020, tweet, she argues:

> *Calling black people who vote for a moderate Dem candidate bc they think white people are most likely to vote for him "low-info," frankly is insulting and feels like a slur. Older black folks vote like this bc they understand things about this country that most of us never will.*

A March 4, 2020, tweet asserts:

> *Forcing people to wait in line for 7 hours to vote is essentially imposing a poll tax as it requires workers to take off the entire*

day to exercise their constitutional right. I'd be curious how
many voters in wealthy, white areas had to wait this long.

Long lines at polls are indeed annoying, but what evidence
supports her idea that the long lines reflect discrimination
against less wealthy and less white precincts?

Trying to find cogent defenses of the 1619 Project in
Hannah-Jones's talks and tweets is a fruitless endeavor.
Similarly, combing through the Twitterverse in search of
wisdom in Hannah-Jones's reactions to the events of the
day is not a rewarding pursuit. It is like combing the tide-
washed sands of Point Comfort for the footprints of those
African captives who passed that way centuries ago.
Close acquaintance with the 1619 Project and especially
Hannah-Jones's observations underscores how so very
little substance has been stretched so very far. The Monáe
commercial, complete with French horn and flowing robe,
is closer to the essence of this marketing venture than
anything Hannah-Jones actually says.

But the rewards for Hannah-Jones's intransigent ignorance have been substantial. On May 4, 2020, the Pulitzer Prize Board awarded her the 2020 Pulitzer Prize for
Commentary for her work on the 1619 Project.[10] After
the riots that tore through American cities in the wake of
the death of George Floyd in police custody, the Claremont Institute's Charles Kesler, writing in the *New York Post*
on June 19, drew a connection between Hannah-Jones's
myth-making and the rhetoric of those who had turned
to arson and looting.[11] Kesler said we could call these the
"1619 Riots," and Hannah-Jones quickly responded by
tweet, owning the phrase: "It would be an honor. Thank
you."[12] On July 8, the film company Lionsgate and Oprah
Winfrey announced a partnership with Hannah-Jones to
turn the 1619 Project into "an expansive portfolio of

films, television series and documentaries, unscripted programming and other forms of entertainment." Hannah-
Jones and Winfrey will be coproducers.[13]

CHAPTER FOUR

1776

THE 1619 PROJECT has attracted critics the way a porchlight attracts moths – and with much the same effect. The light keeps on shining and the moths keep fluttering around it, batting their wings at it pointlessly. The moths in this case are mostly scholars, though there are some who are journalists or independent cultural commentators. The criticisms that have been leveled at the 1619 Project are in many cases valid and, in other circumstances, might be devastating. But the 1619 porchlight goes right on shining, undimmed by the commotion around it.

One reason for that is the *Times'* massive publicity campaign for the project. That campaign reaches millions, whereas the critics can expect to reach at best a few tens of thousands. Such imbalance, however, is only one aspect of the 1619 Project's immunity. The critics are also up against the spirit of triumph – the sheer joy – with which supporters of its core claims have greeted the project. It has been met with popular jubilation of the sort that will not pause merely because some professors have raised issues of factual accuracy. A scholar who points to specific errors is forced to review the context of long-past events and examine details that are unfamiliar to many readers. Those are ineffective tools for planting seeds of doubt among those who have been swept up in exuberant appreciation of the 1619 Project's vast generalizations.

In the early days of the promotional campaign for the project, Hannah-Jones made a point of emphasizing the extraordinarily high standards she set for herself and other contributors. She told one host of a panel discussion, "When you see the finished product you can't really understand all the messiness and ugliness and despair that goes into making it. It was definitely the hardest thing both emotionally and just in terms of the pressure to get it right – not something that would further demean our ancestors; to tell the story the best way and also to understand *every fact had to be right because I knew people were going to come for this reframing.*" Addressing the host, she went on, "When you were saying we are not going to deify our Founders, and the people at the bottom, we were actually going to say, were the most American of all, *you better have your facts right because you know people are going to want to take that down*"[1] (my emphasis).

Hannah-Jones was certainly right to anticipate that her counternarrative of American history would be subject to skeptical review by experts, but her confidence in the factual accuracy of her work was ill-founded. Soon it became clear that many of her assertions were simply false, and some were outrageously false. In this situation, she came to rely on her personal celebrity to avoid dealing with the inaccuracies and on the power of the *Times* to shut out the voices of critics. The critics were left not voiceless but largely unheeded.

Perhaps this would not have happened if we lived at a time when Americans had a better grasp of our history. In the last twenty years, study after study has confirmed the alarming loss of our historical literacy. Fewer than half of American college students in one study could place the Civil War within the correct half century.[2] More than a third of the general public cannot name any rights protected by the First Amendment. Nearly three-quarters of Americans can't name the three branches of government.[3] Only 12 percent of US high school students are scored "proficient" in American history.[4] Many elite colleges and universities fail not only to require their undergraduates to take a course in American history but to require history majors to take one course in American history.

In generations past, children learned such basic facts and a great deal more about American history in grade school, and that learning was reinforced in high school; for those who pursued a college education, it was reinforced through required college courses in American history. But this sort of instruction has been diminished in favor of "social studies" and an educational emphasis on multiculturalism. Thus, a very large number of Americans are ill-equipped to recognize basic factual errors in an account of the American past that sounds, at least superficially, plausible. Politically correct themes get across but not much in the way of learning about the complexities of history. Much of American education has pivoted from teaching to messaging.

POSTMODERN POSTHISTORY

The historians and other critics who point to flaws in the 1619 Project's account of the American past face that barrier as well: fewer people than ever have a basic framework to recognize the validity of the criticism. To this we can add yet another reason why the historians and critics may have a hard time convincing the general public: the rise of academic "postmodernism." This is the idea that almost everything is a matter of interpretation, and few things (or nothing at all) can be resolved by discovering the facts of the matter. A thoroughgoing postmodernist insists that there are no facts, but just "facts," that is, claims that get accepted as true for a while. But any such "fact" is really just someone's assertion, and someone else could assert a different "fact" that would be just as good.

Postmodernism has another facet that is also relevant to the 1619 Project: postmodernism favors the stories told by the "oppressed." It divides society into two parts, the privileged and those whom the privileged exploit. Among the privileges the privileged people enjoy is to tell their own version of history as though it were the absolute truth of what happened in the past. They tell this story to explain and justify their dominant position in society, and they insist on teaching it to those whom they dominate. The poor and oppressed, according to this aspect of postmodernism, rarely get to tell their own versions of history, but they do enjoy a special kind of truth-telling. From the vantage point of being unfairly disadvantaged, they have insight into the lies and self-serving stories told by their oppressors. These insights are necessarily fragmented because the rich and powerful control the main opportunities to build grand and comprehensive accounts of the past. The oppressed often have only unofficial and slightly hidden ways to tell their stories, such as popular songs, folktales, graffiti, and blogs.

The 1619 Project offers a particular version of this kind of postmodernism. The "privileged" in this version are American whites, and their self-serving explanations for their privileged position are a version of history that covers up and excuses the reality of "white supremacy." The 1619 Project aims to unseat white supremacy by bringing forward a powerfully unified version of those insights that black Americans have had all along but have never before had the opportunity to express as a complete narrative. This is what Hannah-Jones means when she blogs that the project will not only reframe the history of America but also reframe "the unparalleled role black people have played in this democracy." The project aims to demolish one version of history and replace it with another crafted to appeal to black pride.

Americans have not embraced postmodernism in its most aggressive form, but it has seeped into popular culture. When people say, "You have your truth, and I have mine," they are acting like good postmodernists. And this sort of argument by sheer assertion has gained tremendous ground though social media, where no one stands as the final arbiter between established truth, mere opinion, and outright fabrication. Instead, we each have our own views, and who is to say that your views are any better than mine? To a large extent these matters don't get settled. Instead they get referred to a circle of like-minded people who support one another and who typically ignore those who hold differing views. Or, if sufficiently aggravated, the like-minded form a digital mob that attacks the dissenter.

We need to keep all of this in mind as we consider what happened when historians and critics began to weigh the factual claims in the 1619 Project.

We also need to keep in mind that, because the 1619 Project is an effort to make slavery the central fact of American history and to elevate racial division over all other considerations, the discussion is fraught with racial sensitivities. Many of the project's most ardent supporters are African-American. Many of its non-African-American supporters are political progressives; others are centrist liberals; and still others conservatives who support the basic idea that American history should be "reframed" in a manner that brings racial division into far greater prominence. Most of the critics themselves defer to this basic idea and present their complaints as efforts to improve the argument of the 1619 Project rather than to discredit it.

But I for one don't think we can take discrediting off the table. How far from the truth can a historical interpretation run before we conclude that it is, fundamentally, a *mis*interpretation?

Hannah-Jones's interpretation of the American Revolution is a case in point.

A SUPPLY OF DOUBTFUL CLAIMS

Several of the historians who have found fault with the 1619 Project have indeed focused on Hannah-Jones's claim that the American Revolution was fought to protect American slave owners from the threat of abolition by the British authorities. Before we turn to their case, however, it is important to note that this interpretation is the first of five main lines of criticism of the 1619 Project that have emerged. The second is Hannah-Jones's contention that Lincoln was a racist whose primary intent was to keep blacks and whites separate; third, her assertion that, "For the most part, black Americans fought back alone"; fourth, the claim advanced most explicitly by 1619 Project contributor Matthew Desmond that plantation slavery was the foundation of American capitalism; and fifth, the thesis of the entire project that the nation's history is best understood as a struggle by American blacks against white supremacy. I deal in later chapters with each of these except the fought-back-alone claim, which I'll dismiss right now. It simply ignores the abolition movement, created and sustained for a century by white Americans. It likewise ignores the huge role of white Americans in the post–Civil War constitutional amendments, and in the civil rights movement. Contrary to what Hannah-Jones contends, black Americans were never alone in their fight against racial injustice. Her declaration on this is the most transparently false of all of her many falsehoods.

These five lines of criticism do not exhaust the 1619 Project's supply of doubtful claims. The project, for example, includes the essays "Why Doesn't the United States Have Universal Health Care? The Answer Begins with Policies Enacted after the Civil War," by Jeneen Interlandi; "A Traffic Jam in Atlanta Would Seem to Have Nothing to Do with Slavery: But Look Closer...," by Kevin M. Kruse; and "Slavery Gave America a Fear of Black People and a Taste for Violent Punishment: Both Still Define Our Criminal-Justice System," by Bryan Stevenson.

Whole books could be written in opposition to any of these claims – and that may well happen in the next few years. But let's say a word about one of the essays that has so far attracted little attention, Wesley Morris's "For Centuries Black Music, Forged in Bondage, Has Been the Sound of Complete Artistic Freedom – No Wonder Everybody Is Always Stealing It." Morris provides an excellent genealogy of how black music for two centuries has influenced and been influenced by other American musical idioms, giving us "the confused thrill of integrated culture."[5] Although he makes the obligatory nods to the *Times'* racial oppression thesis, his essay sings in a different key. It is actually celebratory.

The 1619 Project isn't all bad. It is just wrong in crucial places.

Chapter Four

WHEN INDIGNATION OVERCOMES JUDGMENT

The manner in which Hannah-Jones recounts the story of the American Revolution is as important as the story itself. In the lead article in the magazine, she begins by recounting how her father "always flew an American flag in our front yard."[6] A son of Mississippi sharecroppers, he grew up in segregated Iowa and joined the army at seventeen. After his service, he ended up in menial jobs, and the young Hannah-Jones could not "understand his patriotism." She segues to her learning through "cultural osmosis that the flag wasn't really ours," and that she is heir instead to the horrific history of American slavery. This sets up some of Hannah-Jones's most pungent lines: "Black Americans have also been, and continue to be, foundational to the idea of American freedom." That's because freedom has been so often denied to black Americans, though they deeply understand why it is important and, generation upon generation, seek to fulfill the nation's basic promise. But that promise is elusive: "The United States is a nation founded on both an ideal and a lie." The ideal is that "all men are created equal" and are "endowed by their creator with certain unalienable rights." The lie is the false suggestion that this principle would be applied to black people in America, whose rights had indeed been alienated: "But the white men who drafted those words did not believe them to be true for the hundreds of thousands of black people in their midst."

At this point Hannah-Jones's indignation overcomes her judgment. It was not "men" who drafted those words, but one man in particular. Thomas Jefferson as a slave-holder stands exposed in the judgment of history as a hypocrite, but the question of whether he believed "all men are created equal" is more complicated than that. Could he have believed it and not acted on it?

If we are looking for a man who is utterly consistent in turning his ideals into practice, we won't find him in Jefferson – or perhaps in any man. The ideals that Jefferson gave voice to in the Declaration of Independence, however, reached far beyond the sometimes tawdry circumstances of his life. We have a word for that kind of ideal: transcendent. The principles of the Declaration of Independence transcended the moment and the age in which they were written. They summoned Americans to try harder and for later generations to go further in seeking their fulfillment.

I would suppose that is the reason why Hannah-Jones's father kept that American flag in the front yard and replaced it "as soon as it showed the slightest tatter." He knew what it was about. And he knew it in a way that eludes his daughter.

Having reached the point of the Founders' violent denial of freedom and justice for all, Hannah-Jones turns to the slave Robert Hemmings, who waited on Jefferson when he was in Philadelphia in 1776 for the Continental Congress. Hemmings's presence is a detail worth remembering, but it again prompts Hannah-Jones to an indignant effusion that goes several steps too far: "Enslaved people *were not recognized as human beings* but as property that could be mortgaged, traded, bought, sold, used as collateral, given as a gift and disposed of violently" (emphasis added). Hannah-Jones herself backtracks in the sentence that immediately follows her declaration that enslaved people were not recognized as human beings, writing: "Jefferson's fellow white colonists *knew that black people were human beings*, but they created a network of laws and customs, astounding for both their precision and cruelty, that ensured that enslaved people would never be treated as such" (emphasis added).

In one sentence enslaved blacks "were not recognized" by whites as human beings, and in the very next sentence whites "knew" they "were." What are we to make of this kind of writing?

Possibly it is just carelessness, but it strongly suggests that Hannah-Jones confuses two ideas: the recognition of common humanity and the concept of private property in human beings. The second idea is repellent to modern Americans, and it was distasteful to many Americans of Jefferson's time too. As Americans tend to see it today, slavery "dehumanized" people by treating them as objects and denying their basic human capacities for ties of affection and family connection, and even the capacity to feel pain the way others felt it. Such dehumanizing, of course, went only so far. Slaves resisted; masters recognized that better ways than brute force existed to elicit the desired behavior. In most places, in most times, masters sought to enslave others precisely because of the extreme control it gave them over another person's labor.

The "dehumanizing" view of slavery reflects modern assumptions about humans as first of all individuals whose interior life and sense of self-ownership are primary. Applying this to antebellum slavery may be misleading. People who are captured and forced into slavery are stripped of their original status in the society into which they had been embedded. If we recognize that belonging in a community with its own norms, values, and dense network of relationships is a key aspect of being human, slavery can be seen as a negation of that primary sense of belonging. Note how much this differs from focusing on the slave as a distressed individual. The focus instead is on the despoiling of the prior relationships that comprise cultural identity. The newly enslaved person suffers a social death. But that isn't the end of the story. Slaves, even from disparate origins, soon form their own community with its own norms, values, and dense network of relationships. Hereditary slavery, which dominated in the South, became a culture unto itself. It was a stigmatized culture and slaves were oppressed, but slaves were not "dehumanized" in this other sense.

Slavery was ignominious, not dehumanizing. Among those who suffered the restrictions on personal autonomy imposed by slavery, a very human spirit survived.

The idea that individual human beings had natural rights and that personal freedom was vital to human flourishing often mattered little in the general course of human history, but these ideas began to matter a great deal more in the eighteenth-century British colonies in North America because of an antislavery crusade that was unique in the history of the world. America, contrary to Hannah-Jones, was born not in the midst of indifference to slavery but in the gathering storm of principled opposition to slavery.

The flat contradiction between Hannah-Jones's back-to-back sentences – slaves were *not* recognized as human beings; slaves *were* recognized as human beings – is among the characteristic challenges of her writing. In her zeal to make a strong rhetorical point she often capsizes her argument. Rather than correct the error, she just swims ahead. And what lies ahead is even greater folly.

Chapter Four

AN ASTONISHING CLAIM

In 1776 Jefferson busied himself in Philadelphia in composing a denunciation of Britain's mistreatment of the American colonies. But, says Hannah-Jones, he left out the real reason the colonies are seeking independence: "Conveniently left out of our founding mythology is the fact that one of the primary reasons the colonists decided to declare their independence from Britain was because they wanted to protect the institution of slavery." This is an astonishing claim – astonishing not least to the historians who know the most about the American founding.

One of the first to be astonished – indeed probably the first to read this claim – is a professor of history at Northwestern University, Leslie M. Harris, who is African-American and specializes in American urban history, the African diaspora, and African-American history. On her faculty page she lists her principal research interests as "Pre-Civil War African-American Labor and Social History; History and Historiography of U.S. Slavery; Urban History; Southern History; History of Women, Gender and Sexuality." Her most important book is *In the Shadow of Slavery: African Americans in New York City, 1626–1863*.

Harris was a natural person for the *New York Times* to turn to when the *Times'* fact-checker (name unknown) sought a second opinion on Hannah-Jones's assertion that the colonists were driven to declare their independence in order to preserve slavery. Harris plainly told the fact-checker that the claim was false. We know this because Harris, after six months of public silence, published in *Politico* magazine a bombshell essay, "I Helped Fact-Check the 1619 Project: The *Times* Ignored Me."

The moment of astonishment for Harris came the day after the *Times* launched the 1619 Project. Harris and

[74]

Hannah-Jones had been invited to discuss the project on Georgia Public Radio. Harris writes, "On August 19 of last year I listened in stunned silence as Nikole Hannah-Jones, a reporter for the *New York Times*, repeated an idea that I had vigorously argued against with her fact-checker: that the patriots fought the American Revolution in large part to preserve slavery in North America."[7]

Harris is by no means an opponent of the 1619 Project, which she describes as "a much-needed corrective to the blindly celebratory histories that once dominated our understanding of the past – histories that wrongly suggested racism and slavery were not a central part of U.S. history." Her concern was that factual inaccuracies could jeopardize this important corrective. In particular, she worried that "critics would use the overstated claim" that the Revolution was fought to protect slavery "to discredit the entire undertaking. So far, that's exactly what has happened." Not that this false interpretation of the Revolution is the only problem Harris spotted. She also observed how Hannah-Jones scrambled chronology and erased differences: "In addition, the paper's characterizations of slavery in early America reflected laws and practices more common in the antebellum era than in Colonial times, and did not accurately illustrate the varied experiences of the first generation of enslaved people that arrived in Virginia in 1619." But Harris primarily worried about what would happen when the critics showed up, and her worry came true: "That one sentence about the role of slavery in the founding of the United States has ended up at the center of a debate over the whole project."[8]

Harris takes note of both the "academic historians" who demanded that the *Times* issue corrections and the "emboldened" conservatives who argued that the 1619

Project is "flat-out illegitimate." She mentions a planned "1620 Project" that focused instead on "the Mayflower Landing at Plymouth Rock."[9] Although that was not a reference to my own organization, the National Association of Scholars, in fact the NAS responded the day after the *Times* released its opening salvo with our "1620 Project." And this book bears the title *1620*. While Harris and Hannah-Jones were speaking on Georgia Public Radio, my colleagues and I were discussing how we might answer the *Times'* intent to bypass the long struggle to establish a republic in America founded on the ideals of liberty, equality, and justice.

This is not to say that the history of slavery should be ignored. In fact, one would be hard-pressed to find another historical subject that has produced a greater volume of scholarship over the last half century than slavery. American historians have rightly seen it as a crucial part of our past and a reality that continues to bear on the present. The arguments aren't about the importance of slavery per se, but about how slavery shaped our politics, economics, other social institutions, and cultural life. No valid history can make the entire history of America, from the colonial era, to the republic, through the Civil War, to the present as *only* about slavery or slavery and racism together. That's a gross distortion of our past. And one need not position oneself as "conservative" to see this.

Harris understands this and takes some trouble to find fault with critics who are by no means conservative, such as Gordon Wood and Sean Wilentz. So as not to overtax the reader with examples, I will follow the thread of only these two.

CHAPTER FIVE

1775

W HEN THE HISTORIAN Sean Wilentz pointed to the "cynicism" of the 1619 Project's thesis, his criticism was impossible to ignore. Wilentz is a chaired professor of the American Revolutionary Era at Princeton University. He is the author of numerous books, most pertinently his 2018 work *No Property in Man: Slavery and Antislavery at the Nation's Founding.* He focuses on class and race in the early republic and is widely known for his liberal political views. He won the 2006 Bancroft Prize – the highest award for a historian – for his book *The Rise of American Democracy: Jefferson to Lincoln.*

Wilentz entered the public controversy over the 1619 Project by means of a lecture he gave at the Newark Public Library, in New Jersey, on November 4, 2019. He published the lecture, "American Slavery and 'the Relentless Unforeseen,'" two weeks later in *The New York Review of Books*, perhaps the most prominent journal for the left-leaning intelligentsia in America. Wilentz's major theme in the essay is how the people involved in major historical events have limited knowledge of what is happening around them and no certainty at all about what will follow. History is not a chain of inevitabilities. It is, rather, a struggle among those inspired by different ideals and interests. In retrospect we can see the tide turning in certain conflicts, where one side gains a permanent lead, but that clarity comes only with the passing of considerable time.

Wilentz thus rejects the idea that Emancipation was "preordained," or that human bondage was something that the Western world would inevitably have brought to an end. It ended only because "suddenly, in the late 1740s and early 1750s, Western culture reached a turning point." Western thinkers set off a "moral revolution" focused on finding laws and principles that would bring about a rational order. And this perspective for the first time in human history cast slavery as "a barbaric offense to God, reason, and natural rights."[1]

A few – and at first they were very few – individuals stepped forward to declare that slavery is fundamentally wrong. Wilentz cites the Philadelphia Quaker abolitionist John Woolman, who published an attack on slavery in 1754. Woolman gathered followers, and a network slowly took shape so that by the mid-1770s "a significant number of reformers and intellectuals had come to regard American slavery as pure evil."[2] These abolitionists would eventually prevail, but it would take nearly a hundred years and the horrendous blood-letting of the Civil War to fully realize in the United States the emancipation they sought. They may have succeeded sooner if they had offered step-by-step approaches. Leading abolitionists who argued for immediate and universal emancipation alarmed their countrymen, who feared the abolitionists' apparent desire to level everything.

Wilentz recounts how antislavery politics collided with the popular views of southerners such as South Carolinian Charles Pinckney, who rejected the notion that the Declaration of Independence applied to blacks, slave or free. In light of such feelings, "slavery's defeat was not inevitable." It is only at this point that Wilentz turns his attention to the 1619 Project, which resembles, "ironically, the reactionary proslavery insistence [such as Pinckney's] that the egalitarian self-evident truths of the Declaration were self-evident lies." Wilentz characterizes that view as the "cynicism" that "is on display in *The New York Times Magazine*'s recently launched 1619 Project."[3]

WHAT HANNAH-JONES DOES AND DOES NOT SAY

The linchpin of that cynicism is Nikole Hannah-Jones's essay in which she asserts that "one of the primary reasons the colonists decided to declare independence from Britain was because they wanted to protect the institution of slavery." Wilentz, having spent much of his career studying the actual reasons the colonists decided to declare independence, will have none of this. He goes after Hannah-Jones's supposed evidence for her extraordinary claim. She presents two arguments for this. First:

> *By 1776, Britain had grown deeply conflicted over its role in the barbaric institution that had reshaped the Western Hemisphere. In London there were growing calls to abolish the slave trade. This would have upended the economy of the colonies, in both the North and the South. . . . In other words, we may never have revolted against Britain if the founders had not understood that slavery empowered them to do so; nor if they had not believed that independence was required in order to ensure that slavery would continue.*[4]

The quadruple negatives in that last sentence are a challenge, but Hannah-Jones plainly thinks the Founders saw both a threat to slavery and a slavery-based opportunity to revolt.

Hannah-Jones's second argument is that "there is no mention of slavery in the final Declaration of Independence."[5] Or, she adds, in the Constitution, drafted eleven years later, though various provisions of the Constitution deal with slavery without using the word.

There are two strands of evidence that Hannah-Jones might have brought up in her essay but didn't. These soon emerged in comments by other people. I mention them here to forestall confusion. One is the *Somerset* decision in 1772 by the Court of the King's Bench that outlawed chattel slavery in England and Wales, though not in Britain's overseas holdings. James Somerset was a black slave owned by a British customs officer, who purchased Somerset in Boston. When the customs officer brought him to England, Somerset escaped. He was recaptured, imprisoned, and told he would be resold to a plantation in Jamaica, but his Christian godparents brought suit on his behalf. With the help of Granville Sharp, an abolitionist, Somerset's lawyers argued that English common law did not permit slavery – and the court agreed. There were very few slaves in England, and the ruling thus had little effect. It did not apply to the slave trade in which British merchants and ships continued to participate, and it had no bearing on Britain's overseas colonies.

The other evidence that Hannah-Jones could have cited but did not is Dunmore's Proclamation, issued on November 15, 1775. Dunmore was the royal governor of Virginia. After armed hostilities broke out in the Battles of Lexington and Concord, on April 19, 1775, British authorities began to look for ways to undermine support for the revolutionaries. Dunmore attempted to do this by declaring martial law and offering freedom to indentured servants and slaves who would desert their masters, enlist in the British cause, and bear arms against the revolutionaries. Over the course of the war, an estimated one hundred thousand slaves attempted to escape, but those who enlisted with Dunmore were few. Estimates range from eight hundred to two thousand, and these did not fare well. When Dunmore left Virginia, only three hundred left with him.

WILENTZ'S RESPONSE

Wilentz's response to Hannah-Jones's thesis is straightforward and unequivocal: "this portion of the 1619 Project is simply untrue." The British weren't "'deeply conflicted'" over the slave trade, slavery in the colonies, or slavery in North America.[6] They were complacent. The handful of abolitionists in England had no traction with the public or the government. Wilentz himself introduces the *Somerset* decision and the abolitionist Granville Sharp by way of pointing out how limited that 1772 decision was. Britain had no interest in ending slavery in the colonies, and there was no popular movement to do so. Indeed, no country in the world surpassed Great Britain in the eighteenth century in supplying the Americas with slaves. The crown jewel of its American empire at that time was the slave-based sugar plantation colony of Jamaica. It would import more than one million African slaves during its history, second only to Brazil.

By bringing up a point that could have counted in favor of Hannah-Jones's argument, Wilentz demonstrates how a scrupulous historian goes about the work of weighing the relevant evidence on the other side of the question. The rest of his rather long essay is a detailed account of how the gathering forces of abolition faced off against the defenders of slavery during and after the Revolution. His conclusion: "Revolutionary America, far from a pro-slavery bulwark against the supposedly enlightened British Empire, was a hotbed of antislavery politics, arguably the hottest and most successful of its kind in the Atlantic world prior to 1783."[7]

Wilentz's *New York Review* essay deserves to be read in its entirety, especially by anyone who is inclined to think that Hannah-Jones was just exercising a little interpretive license in making out that the American Revolution was fought to protect slavery. Interpretive license doesn't extend to making up a story that is the dead opposite of the truth.

Wilentz returned to the fray in January 2020 with another long essay, this time in *The Atlantic*. In "A Matter of Facts," Wilentz argues that "no effort to educate the public in order to advance social justice can afford to dispense with a respect for basic facts" – which respect he finds wanting in the 1619 Project. He returns, this time in elaborate detail, to the *Somerset* case and Lord Dunmore's Proclamation, showing how Silverstein, the *Times* magazine editor, had misrepresented them in his reply to the letter from Wilentz and the other historians calling the project's claims into question. As Wilentz observes, "Hannah-Jones's argument is built on partial truths and misstatement of the facts, which combine to impart a fundamentally misleading impression."[8]

GORDON WOOD'S RESPONSE

Gordon Wood, who teaches history at Brown University, is also among the most eminent of American historians. His 1992 book, *The Radicalism of the American Revolution*, won the Pulitzer Prize, and his 1969 book, *The Creation of the American Republic*, won the Bancroft Prize. A more recent work, his 2009 volume in the Oxford History of the United States, *Empire of Liberty: A History of the Early Republic, 1789–1815*, was a finalist for another Pulitzer Prize.

The authority that the *Times* had conferred on Hannah-Jones got Gordon Wood's dander up. A few days after Wilentz's essay appeared in *The New York Review of Books*, the *World Socialist Web Site* posted an interview with Wood.[9] The *what* website? Many on both left and right did a double take when they heard about this. Wood is not known as a socialist, but he was not the first well-known historian to air his dissent from the 1619 Project in this forum. Several editors of the left-wing site began posting articles criticizing the 1619 Project in September 2019, and then turned to posting interviews about it with prominent historians. (Socialist opposition to the 1619 Project is a fascinating crosscurrent in this story that I come back to in chapter 11.)

Wood told the interviewer that he was "surprised" when he saw the *Times* magazine and read Hannah-Jones's essay. His surprise went straight to her claims "that the Revolution occurred primarily because of the Americans' desire to save their slaves." His worry, he says, is that the 1619 Project is "going to become the basis for high school education and has the authority of the *New York Times* behind it, and yet it is so wrong in so many ways." The interviewer presses the point about the *Times'* failure to seek the counsel of "one of the foremost authorities on the American Revolution." Wood affirms he was not approached and adds, "None of the leading scholars of the whole period from the Revolution to the Civil War, as far as I know, have been consulted."[10]

In the interview, Wood explains that, at the time the Constitution was written, "nearly everybody knew" that slavery was "a barbaric thing" and wrongly assumed it was "on the road to extinction." It is the American Revolution that makes slavery "a problem for the world." Without the Revolution, slavery would have continued in the British Empire indefinitely. The British didn't "get around to freeing the slaves in the West Indies until 1833," and would not have done it then either except that West Indian planters could no longer call on Southern support. Wood bats aside Hannah-Jones's central claim: "I just don't think there is much evidence for it, and in fact the contrary is more true to what happened. The Revolution unleashed antislavery sentiments that led to the first abolition movements in the history of the world."[11]

Gordon Wood's displeasure with the 1619 Project didn't stop there. As noted in chapter 2, he was one of the five historians (the others being Wilentz, Victoria Bynum, James McPherson, and James Oakes) who wrote to the *Times* to urge the editors to correct several factual errors that the project was propagating. The first of these errors is Hannah-Jones's assertion about the cause of the American Revolution. The letter states:

> *On the American Revolution, pivotal to any account of our history, the project asserts that the founders declared the colonies' independence of Britain "in order to ensure slavery would continue." This is not true. If supportable, the allegation would be astounding – yet every statement offered by the project to validate it is false.*

The five historians anticipated that the *Times* might call this just a matter of interpretation, so they added: "These errors, which concern major events, cannot be described as interpretation or 'framing.' They are matters of verifi-

able fact, which are the foundation of both honest scholarship and honest journalism."[12]

Silverstein replied at some length but evaded the substance of the historians' letter and ended up declaring,
exactly as the historians feared, that it is all a matter of
interpretation. Among the editor's observations: "Historical understanding is not fixed. Within the world of
academic history, differing views exist, if not over what
precisely happened, then about why it happened, who
made it happen, how to interpret the motivations of historical actors and what it all means."[13]

He defends Hannah-Jones's peculiar account of the
American Revolution by citing David Waldstreicher,
Alfred W. Blumrosen and Ruth G. Blumrosen, and Jill
Lepore as upholding the idea that some American slave-
holders had some "uneasiness" about the "growing anti-
slavery movement in Britain." In fact there was no such
movement, but it had now become important for the
Times to discover some shred of credibility for the idea.
Waldstreicher is a professor of history at the Graduate
Center of the City University of New York and the author
of several books on slavery, including *Slavery's Constitution:
From Revolution to Ratification* (2009) and *Runaway America:
Benjamin Franklin, Slavery, and the American Revolution* (2004).
The Blumrosens were civil rights attorneys and law professors who published *Slave Nation: How Slavery United the
Colonies and Sparked the American Revolution* (2005). Lepore,
a historian at Harvard, has recently published *These
Truths: A History of the United States* (2018), which includes
a single sentence crediting Dunmore's Proclamation
(offering the slaves of Patriots their freedom if they joined
the British forces) as tipping "the scales in favor of American independence."[14]

Chapter Five

On the authority of Silverstein, we can say that Hannah-Jones didn't make up her thesis out of thin air. Though she didn't cite Waldstreicher, the Blumrosens, or Lepore, these writers offer the precedent of having indulged similar surmises.

Silverstein's reply (published on December 20, 2019, and updated on January 4, 2020) offered no corrections to the 1619 Project essays. Gordon Wood, however, did not let the matter go. He responded with a public letter to Silverstein, reiterating that he has "no quarrel with the idea behind the project." Paying more attention to "the importance of slavery in the history of our country is essential." But Wood's displeasure with the factual sloppiness of the 1619 Project reaches a new level in his letter. The "interpretations" the project puts forward are "perverse and distorted." He adds, "We all want justice, but not at the expense of truth." Wood quotes Hannah-Jones's thesis yet again and demolishes it:

> *I don't know of any colonist who said that they wanted independence in order to preserve their slaves. No colonist expressed alarm that the mother country was out to abolish slavery in 1776. If southerners were concerned about losing their slaves, why didn't they make efforts to ally with the slaveholding planters in the British West Indies?*

And he goes on: "Far from preserving slavery the North saw the Revolution as an opportunity to abolish the institution. The first anti-slave movements in the history of the world, supported by whites as well as blacks, took place in the northern states in the years immediately following 1776."[15] He couldn't have made it any plainer.

Wood was still not done attacking the veracity of the project in general and Hannah-Jones's the-Revolution-was-fought-to-protect-slavery thesis in particular. In February 2020, reviewing Mary Beth Norton's book *1774* in the *Wall Street Journal*, Wood begins by launching some arrows at the 1619 Project and Silverstein's defense of it. Wood seems especially intent on deflating Lepore's hapless sentence about the importance of Dunmore's Proclamation, which Silverstein had marshaled in support. Norton's book "shows conclusively that the scales had been tipped [Lepore's metaphor] in favor of independence long before Dunmore issued his proclamation." He concludes the review by hammering that nail one more time. "And never in [Norton's] detailed account of that long year does she declare that the protection of slavery had anything to do with bringing about independence."[16]

THE TIMES RETREATS — A BIT

On March 11, 2020, after seven months of battering by historians, the *Times* retreated a tiny bit. Prompted by the revelation five days earlier by Leslie Harris that her fact-checking for the *Times* had been ignored, Silverstein posted "An Update to The 1619 Project," in which he offered "a clarification to a passage" in Hannah-Jones's essay. Referring to Hannah-Jones's statement that "one of the primary reasons the colonists decided to declare their independence from Britain was because they wanted to protect the institution of slavery," Silverstein said that the *Times* recognizes that some readers may have interpreted this to mean that "protecting slavery was a primary motivation for *all* of the colonists." The wording has now been changed to say "some of" the colonists.[17]

This surely puts the *Times* on technically safe ground. If there were only two colonists out of the roughly 2.5 million in 1776 who believed that they should rebel against the British government because Britain might one day abolish slavery, the new sentence would be accurate. But of course the *Times* means to imply a great deal more than that. The insinuation is that the historians who complained were picking on an errant detail, and that fear of Britain emancipating American slaves really was a major factor in the American Revolution. Other than Lepore in one incorrect sentence, which she backed away from, no reputable historian believes this as a characterization of the Revolution as a whole, and only one major historian – whom we will come to shortly – sees it as a factor in Virginia.

But the *Times* is still determined to uphold its thesis, or as Silverstein puts it in the notice, "We stand behind the basic point, which is that among the various motivations that drove the patriots toward independence was a concern that the British would seek or were already seeking to disrupt in various ways the entrenched system of American slavery."[18] That rephrasing, of course, climbs down from Hannah-Jones's "one of the primary reasons." Silverstein tries to nuance his way to safer ground like a man trying to find his footing in a bog. The problem is that the one time the British showed any interest in disrupting American slavery – Dunmore's Proclamation – came six months after the Battles of Lexington and Concord, which were themselves the outcome of a profound disaffection with British rule that had been gathering strength for years.

The Stamp Act passed in March 1765. The Boston Massacre was in March 1770. The Boston Tea Party, executed by the Sons of Liberty, was in December 1773. Not so long ago, every American schoolchild knew what these events were and how they led up to the Revolution. While there is room to debate how the "the various motivations that drove the patriots toward independence" should be weighed next to one another and how they came together to spark an armed rebellion, there is no room at all to change the chronology and teleport Dunmore's Proclamation into the period when revolutionary sentiment was building.

A small case can be made that Dunmore's Proclamation further inflamed slave owners in Virginia, but intensifying an ongoing rebellion is pretty far from "one of the primary reasons" for the Revolution.

Does Silverstein have anything more than this to buttress his now weaker version of Hannah-Jones's claim? Yes, and we need to pay attention to it.

VIRGINIA'S DISCONTENTS

Silverstein does not go into any detail, but he invokes "the past 40 years or so of early American historiography" as paying attention to "the role of slavery and the agency of enslaved people in driving events of the Revolutionary period."[19] He cites only one historian, Alan Taylor, who teaches at the University of Virginia, and whose works include the 2014 Pulitzer Prize–winning book *The Internal Enemy: Slavery and War in Virginia, 1772–1832*.

Hannah-Jones never referred to Taylor, nor did Silverstein mention him in his earlier defense of Hannah-Jones's essay. Regardless of whether they knew of Taylor when the 1619 Project was being written or he came to their attention later, he is highly relevant.

Taylor's book focuses on the War of 1812, but he devotes a chapter to the Revolution, in which he does indeed say some things that fit with Hannah-Jones's thesis. He writes, for example, that the *Somerset* decision was "widely reported in the American press" and "caused a sensation." And, "Virginia's leaders feared that Parliament might eventually legislate against slavery in America."[20] This is eye-opening, but Taylor's evidence for these hetero-dox views is thin. He cites the Blumrosens and Wald-streicher, and three other sources: George William Van Cleve's *A Slaveholders' Union: Slavery, Politics, and the Constitution in the Early Republic* (2010), Seymour Drescher's *Abolition: A History of Slavery and Antislavery* (2009), and Christopher Leslie Brown's *Moral Capital: Foundations of British Abolitionism* (2006).

These three books are dubious props for Taylor's argument. Van Cleve's comes closest to supporting Taylor's claim in depicting the restlessness of Virginia planters under British rule, but it does not suggest they acted out of fear that Britain would end slavery in the colony. Rather, says Van Cleve, the planters worried that "diminished imperial protection for slavery" might threaten their "property rights" in other colonies that were less friendly to slavery. They sought "local autonomy" over slavery to stave off this prospect – which would definitely not explain the willingness of Virginia or the other southern colonies to join with the northern colonies where the abolitionist movement had already made major gains. The Revolution, in Van Cleve's view, far from protecting slavery, "posed a series of important additional threats to slavery."[21]

Drescher recounts how "Parliament recoiled at the suggestion" of William Lyttelton in October 1775 that the British should foment slave rebellions in the southern colonies. He also cites Edmund Burke's scorn for Dunmore's tactic of inviting American slaves to desert their masters.[22] He reports nothing that would give a foundation to a fear by Americans that the British were contemplating an end to American slavery, and he reports no instances of such fears on the part of Americans.

Brown shows at length and in detail that the British antislavery movement began *after* the American Revolution, concluding: "The British antislavery movement that began in the late 1780s was, therefore, a late-born sibling in the family of Anglo-American antislavery campaigns."[23]

But Taylor paints a different picture. "When confronted by any sign of slave discontent," he writes, "Virginians anticipated a ripening into bloody rebellion." He says the slaveholding Virginians of the pre-revolutionary era lived in terror of a slave uprising, and almost any British action could be peered at through that lens. Virginia was eager to stop further imports of slaves because it already had a large surplus. The British government, however, blocked that effort, and Virginians, including Jefferson, saw this as further destabilizing an already perilous situation. Taylor argues that Virginia's peculiar concerns were an ingredient in the American Revolution comparable to the events in Massachusetts: "The traditional history of the American Revolution emphasizes the role of Massachusetts in resisting British taxes, but Virginia proved equally important to the Patriot coalition."[24] Taylor is a serious historian whose words have to be considered carefully, particularly when his thinking runs counter to what other historians have said; but on this matter his sourcing for his claims falls far short of supporting them.

There are three main problems with Taylor's argument. First, the authorities he cites say little that backs up his contention that the *Somerset* decision "caused a sensation" in Virginia. There is some speculation in some of his cited sources, but no evidence, and Taylor himself cites none. He tells us that "colonial masters felt shocked by the implication that their property system defied English traditions of liberty," but we don't see or hear from any

of these shocked slaveholders, let alone see them trans-
lating that shock into taking up arms against England.
The only contemporary who is named is an Englishman
named Ambrose Serle, who mocks the slaveholders as
hating "absolute rule" by others when they "ardently
pursue it for themselves."[25] Serle was a senior clerk who
worked in the British department of the secretary of
state, had traveled in America, and wrote a tract titled
Americans against Liberty, in which he upheld the virtues of
the enlightened English over the backward Americans.
Quoted by Brown, who devotes several pages to the
pompous clerk, Serle emerges not as an advocate of abolition but as a champion of British imperial rule.

Strong heterodox claims require strong evidence – or
at least *some* evidence, and Taylor appears to come up
empty on this point. He is much more convincing about
white Virginians' fear of slave revolts, and, as the Revolution got underway, the British adroitly exploited this fear.
Perhaps at that point some Virginians remembered the
Somerset decision, but it would be good to see actual evidence of that too.

Second, there is the general issue of how Virginia participated in the events leading up to the Revolution. The
record is clear that the public debates in Virginia over
British control were dominated by other matters and by
men whose interests were broader than possible British
emancipation of slaves. George Washington opposed
British colonial policies from at least 1754, when he was
passed over for promotion to the status of a British officer after his service in the French and Indian War. Washington realized then that Americans, no matter their
accomplishments, would never be treated by the British
as equals. The principle of equality mattered deeply to
him. After his election to Virginia's House of Burgesses

in 1759 – long before the *Somerset* decision – Washington expressed the displeasure of Virginia planters over Britain's limits on westward expansion. Virginia's unhappiness with British rule soon took the shape of seeking alliances with the other colonies. In May 1774, Virginia proposed a congress of all the colonies, and Virginia's Peyton Randolph was elected president of the first Continental Congress, to which Washington was a delegate. Washington was named commander in chief of the Continental Army on June 19, 1775. None of this would have been possible if the northern colonies had seen Virginia as driven by a panic at the prospect of losing its slaves.

Third, historians other than Taylor see no such panic. As Gordon Wood observes, Dunmore's Proclamation "may have tipped the scales for some hesitant Virginia planters, but by then the revolutionary movement was already well along in Virginia." And: "Perhaps some southern slaveholders were alarmed by news of the *Somerset* decision, but we don't have any evidence of that." Moreover, says Wood:

> *There is no evidence in 1776 of a rising movement to abolish the Atlantic slave trade, as the 1619 Project erroneously asserts, nor is there any evidence the British government was eager to do so. But even if either were the case, ending the Atlantic slave trade would have been welcomed by the Virginia planters, who already had more slaves than they needed. Indeed, the Virginians in the years following independence took the lead in moving to abolish the despicable international slave trade.*[26]

Sean Wilentz disputes the point even more vigorously, taking Taylor's word, "sensation," and throwing it back at the supporters of this view:

Chapter Five

In fact, the Somerset *ruling caused no such sensation. In the entire slaveholding South, a total of six newspapers – one in Maryland, two in Virginia, and three in South Carolina – published only 15 reports about* Somerset, *virtually all of them very brief. Coverage was spotty: The two South Carolina newspapers that devoted the most space to the case didn't even report its outcome. American newspaper readers learned far more about the doings of the queen of Denmark, George III's sister Caroline, whom Danish rebels had charged with having an affair with the court physician and plotting the death of her husband. A pair of Boston newspapers gave the* Somerset *decision prominent play; otherwise, most of the coverage appeared in the tiny-font foreign dispatches placed on the second or third page of a four- or six-page issue.*

Above all, Wilentz continues,

the reportage was almost entirely matter-of-fact, betraying no fear of incipient tyranny. A London correspondent for one New York newspaper did predict, months in advance of the actual ruling, that the case "will occasion a greater ferment in America (particularly in the islands) than the Stamp Act," but that forecast fell flat. Some recent studies have conjectured that the Somerset *ruling must have intensely riled southern slaveholders, and word of the decision may well have encouraged enslaved Virginians about the prospects of their gaining freedom, which could have added to slaveholders' constant fears of insurrection. Actual evidence, however, that the* Somerset *decision jolted the slaveholders into fearing an abolitionist Britain – let alone to the extent that it can be considered a leading impetus to declaring independence – is less than scant.*

Wilentz has more to say on this than I can conveniently quote. He allows that Dunmore's Proclamation, after the war had started, "likely stiffened the resolve for independence among the rebel patriots whom Dunmore singled out, but they were already rebels." Plainly, it "cannot be held up as evidence that the slaveholder colonists wanted to separate from Britain to protect the institution of slavery."[27]

The evidence adduced by Van Cleve, in *A Slaveholders' Union*, simply does not line up with Taylor's generalizations. Van Cleve provides one of the richest and most detailed accounts of colonial debates about slavery in this era, including reactions to the *Somerset* decision. He observes that twenty-two of twenty-four surviving colonial newspapers "contained reports of the [*Somerset*] arguments, an account of the decision, or both." An anonymous South Carolinian circulated a pamphlet citing *Somerset* as a reason why the delegate to the First Continental Congress should not, as Van Cleve puts it, "adopt all English liberties." Henry Marchant, a Rhode Island official who as an attorney represented a slaveholder's interests, inveighed against *Somerset* in his private diary as providing a "'plausible pretense'" to "cheat an honest American of his slave."[28]

Having scoured the record, Van Cleve finds that "American slaveholders reacted to *Somerset* either with criticism or with public silence," which is to say *not* with determination to overthrow British authority in order to preserve slavery. Apropos of silence, Van Cleve cites the correspondence of Peleg Clarke, a Newport, Rhode Island, slave-ship captain who in the aftermath of the *Somerset* decision never mentions it. Van Cleve writes, "Clarke and his correspondents in England and the West Indies believed that African slave prices and American molasses prices then had the largest impact on the trade."[29] The *Somerset* decision didn't even warrant a shrug from this slave trader.

Chapter Five

I cannot reconcile Wilentz's count of the number of newspapers (six) that reported on *Somerset* with Van Cleve's count (22), except that Van Cleve included northern newspapers. But these are the sorts of details that historians have to hash out. Disagreement among historians, all of them expert on the period and the topic, is normal. It doesn't mean the truth is unattainable. Disagreements lead the way to close, and closer, examination of possible sources and the winnowing out of misleading impressions and premature or mistaken conclusions.

On the most generous interpretation, what the 1619 Project has done is pick sides in a scholarly dispute initially without citing sources and then consistently without acknowledging that the experts have sharply different views. After months of standing pat behind the *Times'* original declaration that America launched the revolution in order to preserve slavery, Jake Silverstein began backfilling the holes in the 1619 argument with the names of historians who supposedly upheld Hannah-Jones's thesis – but even then, it appears that no one at the *Times* took the trouble to examine these sources closely, or even cursorily.

Historians argue among themselves by digging deeper and deeper into archives in search of decisive evidence. The *Times*, by contrast – at least in this case – attempted to settle such a dispute by fiat. That is not the legitimate role of a newspaper. The balance of evidence at this point favors the standard interpretation of the causes of the American Revolution, in which the fear that the British would abolish slavery in the American colonies played no part at all.

1775

DAYLIGHT?

I began the previous chapter by observing that criticisms of the 1619 Project seem as futile as moths beating their wings against a porchlight. But a porchlight left on till morning seems rather dim in daylight.

The focus of this chapter is the 1619 Project's assertion that the American Revolution came about because the colonists were eager to perpetuate slavery and feared that the British would take it away. Some historians credit this idea: Waldstreicher, the Blumrosens, Lepore (perhaps), and Taylor among them. But many of the most prominent historians do not. The weight of expert opinion testifies against the *Times*.

Recognizing this, the *Times* magazine's editor in chief has gone from merely brushing aside the strictures of the nation's leading historians to attempting to rescue Hannah-Jones's idea by diluting it. Having replied to the letter from five historians, including Sean Wilentz and Gordon Wood, with a fairly lengthy if evasive answer, Silverstein took a different tack when a follow-up letter from twelve more major historians criticized the project's claim: this was met with his more abrupt determination that "no corrections are warranted."[30] (Note that the *Times* magazine declined to print the twelve historians' letter, though Silverstein did reply to it.) But immediately following Leslie Harris's revelation that the *Times* had ignored her when she clearly told its fact-checker in advance of the project's publication that Hannah-Jones's thesis is false, then – and only then – did Silverstein feel moved to make a correction.

Is public shaming the only force strong enough to overcome the *Times*' inertia? Can we make up any story we want, regardless of the evidence, and declare that we are just "reframing" history?

It suits the agenda of the 1619 Project to make all of American history a story about slavery. The American Revolution, as one of the major events that had very little to do with the institution of slavery, appears to stand in the way of that agenda. The way to solve this problem, hit upon by Hannah-Jones, was to impose a radical new interpretation on the Revolution that made it centrally about slavery after all. It is clear that this interpretation – even if Alan Taylor's reading of the situation in Virginia were to stand up to the skepticism of his colleagues – rests on "less than scant" (to borrow Wilentz's phrase) historical evidence. Hannah-Jones's ideological zeal outran her fidelity to the truth.

The *Times* pushed ahead with this fable with the assistance of the Pulitzer Center, thousands of eagerly supportive schoolteachers, and a contingent of academic historians who may know the story is false but who see the larger cause of pursuing racial justice as overriding the need for historical accuracy – and still others who fear being labeled "racist" if they speak out.

Still, let's trust that day will eventually dawn and spoil the magical illusions of the porchlight. At some point, perhaps years from now, real history will be as plain as day. Until then, we have the 1619 Project.

CHAPTER SIX

MARCH 2020

IN MID-MARCH 2020, as I worked on this book, I had a stack of 138 articles that had been published to that point either supporting or criticizing the 1619 Project. I was surely missing some, but not many. As a rough measure of public influence, 138 responses strikes me as a low number. Even a minor adjustment in immigration rules or a tweak to the tax codes elicits many times that number of articles in a single week. But a friend of mine who works on cultural issues views the size of the response as a triumph. For criticism of a major move by the cultural left, he said to me, "this is as good as it gets."

In chapter 3, I characterized the 1619 Project as a media event and traced the way the *New York Times* staged it. In this chapter I describe – briefly – the project's opponents, and somewhat more fully the forces allied to or sympathetic with the 1619 Project. To understand how the controversy plays out, we need a *dramatis personae*. As anyone who goes to the theater knows, the list of characters in the program is awfully handy to have.

THE OPPOSITION

As part of my work for the National Association of Scholars, I speak to groups of people around the country

Chapter Six

interested in controversies in education. Recently, I have been asking for a show of hands to the question, "Have you heard of the 1619 Project?" In Columbia, South Carolina; Palm Springs, California; and Phoenix, Arizona, few hands went up. And these were groups of people self-selected for their interests in history and education. If I were to judge by that small sample, the 1619 Project would not seem to have registered strongly with the American public.

America, of course, is a big place, and lack of attention to an issue in some quarters can be offset by fervent enthusiasm in others. Much of the energetic interest so far has come from those who believe the 1619 Project is a major step in the right direction. We critics, on the other hand, have been searching for ways to galvanize public opposition. The National Association of Scholars has been recording interviews with scholars and publishing articles. So, too, has the International Committee of the Fourth International on its *World Socialist Web Site*. Robert Woodson, founder of the Woodson Center, has assembled "a consortium of top black academics, columnists, social service providers, business leaders and clergy from across America" who are critical of the 1619 Project. The Woodson Center calls its initiative "1776 Unites," and is "committed to telling the complete history of America and black Americans from 1776 to [the] present."

The American Institute for Economic Research, a free-market-oriented think tank in Great Barrington, Massachusetts, has taken an active interest in critiquing the 1619 Project, as have some other libertarian entities such as *Reason* magazine and the Liberty Fund (based in Indianapolis), through its publication *Law & Liberty*. The criticisms of the 1619 Project from the free-market-oriented segment of the political spectrum are wide-ranging but focus especially on the claims of the *Times*' contributors who trace American capitalism and American prosperity to black slavery.

The Claremont Institute, based in the Los Angeles area, focuses on "restoring the principles of the American Founding to their rightful, preeminent authority in our national life." It opposes the 1619 Project as a threat to public understanding of and support for those principles. In February 2020, the Heritage Foundation, the prominent conservative think tank in Washington, DC, held a summit of leaders from a dozen groups opposed to the 1619 Project. Though not united on strategy and tactics, the participants share a common foundation of concern among right-of-center groups that pay attention to education. Among these are the Ashbrook Center (Ohio), the RealClear family of websites, the Bill of Rights Institute (Virginia), the Texas Public Policy Foundation, and the Manhattan Institute.

The powers of this diverse assembly of opponents to the 1619 Project have yet to be fully tested. Beginning in March, the nation's schools were mostly shut down in response to the coronavirus pandemic, and national attention was focused on shelter-in-place edicts, a shortage of face masks, emergency medical supplies, diagnostic tests, treatments, infection and mortality rates, catastrophic declines in the stock market, job losses, and economic disaster. The public mind was not on the 1619 Project, and the only history that was getting attention was the history of past epidemics.

The longer-term consequences of this Great Pause in American life are still unknowable. But the *New York Times*' effort to "reframe" all of American history has been energized by the discontent. The 1619 Project offered itself as one way to channel the pain of the economic dislocations into racial resentment and white guilt. After the death of George Floyd in police custody in Minneapolis in late May 2020, the nation experienced a paroxysm of protests that in many cases escalated into riots and murders.

Hannah-Jones proceeded to justify these riots as an appropriate response to black oppression. In one interview on national television, she cautioned, "I think we need to be very careful with our language. Yes, it is disturbing to see property being destroyed, it's disturbing to see people taking property from stores, but these are things. And violence is when an agent of the state kneels on a man's neck until all of the life is leached out of his body. Destroying property, which can be replaced, is not violence. And to put those things – to use the same language to describe those two things I think really – it's not moral to do that."[1]

This was not a one-off remark by Hannah-Jones. On another network, she elaborated, "I think I would not describe looting as violence. Looting is property damage, but it is not violence." Telling the interviewer she wanted "to go to Martin Luther King's own words," she quoted and paraphrased parts of a speech (which she calls a "letter") he gave in 1967, to the effect that "looting comes from the most enraged and deprived Negro and allows them to take hold of consumer goods with the ease that a white man does by using his purse. Often, the Negro does not even want what he takes. He wants the experience of taking. Negroes have committed crimes, but they are the derivative crimes, and they are born of the greater crimes of the white society. So, when we ask Negroes to abide by the law, let us also demand that the white man abide by the law in the ghettos as well. So, I think we need to have some perspective on what exactly we're seeing when we call that violence and looting."[2]

In Hannah-Jones's view, the riots stemmed from the long history of white oppression of blacks in America. She made no mention of the fact that, in many of the riots, a majority of the rioters were in fact white or that the violence was often instigated by members of mostly white radical activist groups such as Antifa.[3] Be that as it may, Hannah-Jones succeeded in framing the riots as the fulfillment of the diagnosis she offered in the 1619 Project. Recall that when Charles Kesler dubbed the attacks the "1619 Riots," Hannah-Jones quickly and gratefully accepted the label.[4]

At this point – I am writing in July 2020 – the violence and destruction of the riots, the 1619 Project, and a third element – a consuming hatred of President Trump by many on the political left – have converged into a hysteria that sees itself as a righteous response to an omnipresent evil in American life. A 1619-derived demand for "anti-racism" as a new way of life has emerged as a penitential cult – a religion of shame – embraced by hundreds of college presidents, corporate boards, and political leaders.

How much that penitential cult can be traced directly to the 1619 Project is open to debate. The next most obvious contributor is the historian Ibram X. Kendi. It is a close question how much Hannah-Jones drew from Kendi, and as close a question of how much Kendi benefited from the *Times'* effort to give saturation coverage to antiracism initiatives. Kendi's *Stamped from the Beginning: The Definitive History of Racist Ideas in America*, winner of the 2016 National Book Award, plainly stands in the background of the 1619 Project. Hannah-Jones cites no sources, but Kendi's massive book covers much of the same material as the 1619 Project.

Moreover, Kendi's follow-on book, *How to Be an Anti-racist*, was released the same month as the 1619 Project,

and ballyhooed weeks before its release by the *Times'*
"culture reporter," Jennifer Schuessler. Schuessler announced, "it's a book that, like its predecessor, seems to
be arriving at exactly the right moment, as President
Trump's verbal attacks on lawmakers of color and on the
city of Baltimore have spurred both intense outrage and
debate on how to respond."[5] Two days after the *Times*
published the 1619 Project, it ran a fuller review of *How
to Be an Antiracist.* The reviewer, Jeffrey C. Stewart, called
it "the most courageous book to date on the problem of
race in the Western mind."[6] Kendi's work plainly dove-
tails with Hannah-Jones's project, and in December 2019
the two of them appeared together on the podcast *Why
Is This Happening?*, hosted by MSNBC's Chris Hayes.[7]

The intensity of the 1619 delirium drowns out the
many cogent criticisms of the 1619 Project itself, but the
intensity is bound to be short-lived. Even if its proponents prevail in the marketplace and in politics, the
movement will necessarily subside. Millenarian fantasies,
including the fantasy that American society will reorga-
nize itself as a permanent system of reparations for slavery, always give way to disappointing reality in the end.
But that end is not yet. The energy of the 1619 Project has
not dissipated. Too many people – including Oprah – have
too much invested in its success for it to fade out soon.

THE PROMOTERS

With the *New York Times* taking the lead in promoting its
own work, one might think there would be less impetus
for other supporters to organize and come forward. But
in fact the 1619 Project has assembled a formidable army
of supporting groups. The Pulitzer Center partnered
with the *Times* in advance of the August 18 magazine

debut and announced its role, a program called "The 1619 Project in Schools," on the inside back cover. Since then, the Pulitzer Center has taken the lead in getting the 1619 Project curriculum into schools, which appears to be the primary goal of the whole project. I devote a later chapter to describing that curriculum. First, let's take a census of who is pushing it.

The National Education Association (NEA), the nation's largest teachers' union, with more than three million members in more than fourteen thousand communities, announced that it "recently worked with *The New York Times* to distribute copies of The 1619 Project to educators and activists around the country to help give us a deeper understanding of systemic racism and its impact."[8] The NEA's "EdJustice" program maintains a "1619 Project Resource Page," with links to "1619 Project Curriculum" from the Pulitzer Center as well as links to other resources, including the Southern Poverty Law Center's (SPLC) project "Teaching Tolerance," and a group called Black Lives Matter at School.

It isn't clear that Black Lives Matter at School has officially endorsed the 1619 Project, but the two frequently intertwine. For example, when the group D.C. Area Educators for Social Justice (or Social Change – both names are used) sponsored an event for teachers called "Black Lives Matter at School Week of Action Curriculum Fair" on January 21, 2020, teachers were offered a copy of the "1619 Project booklet."[9] In examining support for the 1619 Project, no matter where you start, you can follow the threads to many groups that have overlapping political agendas.

That "1619 Project booklet" distributed by the same D.C. Area Educators group, for example, is a publication of the Zinn Education Project, named for the late

Howard Zinn, a radical Marxist historian best known for his book *A People's History of the United States.* In December 2019, the Zinn Education Project began to offer assistance with "Teaching with *New York Times* 1619 Project."[10] D.C. Area Educators for Social Justice bills itself as part of Teaching for Change, which in turn is a thirty-year-old group of progressive activists that aims to build "social justice starting in the classroom."[11] Teaching for Change collaborates with a group called Rethinking Schools and the Zinn Education Project to bring Zinn's *People's History* "to the classroom."[12]

Rethinking Schools in turn "grew out of" an organizing effort among Milwaukee public school teachers in 1986 to become "a nationally prominent publisher of educational materials." Those materials focus on "the creation of a humane, caring, multiracial democracy. While writing for a broad audience, Rethinking Schools emphasizes problems facing urban schools, particularly issues of race."[13] As far as I can tell, Rethinking Schools hasn't fully caught up with the 1619 Project, but it works on closely aligned themes. In March 2019, it published *Teaching a People's History of Abolition and the Civil War*, edited by Adam Sanchez. Sanchez offers ten "classroom-tested lessons" aimed at debunking the idea that Lincoln freed the slaves and focusing instead on the "heroic actions of the enslaved themselves."[14] Sanchez's view matches perfectly with Hannah-Jones's assessment that Lincoln was a racist who "opposed black equality" and who blamed the slaves themselves for the war.[15]

The Zinn Education Project lists Sanchez's book as one of its recommended "Teaching Resources on 1619 Project Themes." This collection of materials generally predates the 1619 Project, but the Zinn curators have not misjudged its relevance to the project. The items match the 1619 Project very closely in substance and in spirit. As presented on the Zinn website, they include:

- *The Color Line. Teaching Activity. By Bill Bigelow. A lesson on the countless colonial laws enacted to create division and inequality based on race. This helps students understand the origins of racism in the United States and who benefits.*

- *Constitution Role Play. Through role-play, upend the traditional narrative of the Constitutional Convention by including the perspectives of workers, enslaved people, and poor farmers, alongside those of the real participants – the white wealthy elite.*

- *Missing from Presidents' Day: The People They Enslaved*

- *How to Make Amends: A Lesson on Reparations*

These threads get confusing, so let me recapitulate. I noted that the nation's largest teachers' union, the NEA, worked with the *Times* to distribute copies of the 1619 Project, and to this end worked with the Pulitzer Center, the Southern Poverty Law Center, and Black Lives Matter at School. Putting aside the Pulitzer Center and the SPLC for the moment, I followed Black Lives Matter at School, which led to other groups: Teaching for Change, the Zinn Education Project, and Rethinking Schools – all of which had their own links and affinities to the 1619 Project. With these groups, we are in the cultural Marxist, radical anti-American end of the pool, where the goal is to indoctrinate American children with a hatred of their country. A substantial portion of that indoctrination is the effort to instill racial animosity and the conviction among African Americans that they are now and have always been the victims of systemic racial oppression.

This is the soil out of which the 1619 Project grew. Some of the invective preceded the *New York Times*' effort to make a grand statement; some followed it. When it was published, the activists immediately recognized it as part and parcel of an existing line of advocacy, and they took it and ran with it.

Much of this played out on a local level. D.C. Area Educators for Social Change was connected to a local branch of Black Lives Matter at School, but that body was connected with radical teachers in many other school districts as well. In January 2020, a Milwaukee teachers' union, MTEA, promoted Milwaukee Black Lives Matter at School National Action Week with a campaign that likewise touted the 1619 Project.[16] So did the California Teachers Association, which provided the trifecta of Black Lives Matter at School, the Zinn Education Project, and the 1619 Project.[17]

A little bit of googling will reveal to anyone who is curious that this pattern is widespread among teachers' unions and among radicalized teachers across the country. But a teacher need not be radicalized to be drawn by the allure of the 1619 Project. It can look to the unwary as merely a convenient way to show support for black students and to signal one's own antiracist attitudes.

THE PULITZER CENTER

The Pulitzer Center is the *Times*' primary partner in turning the 1619 Project from a journalistic stunt into an educational reality. It's important to note that, though the Pulitzer Center shares a famous name with the Pulitzer Prizes, those come from an entirely different body. The Pulitzer Prizes were created by the nineteenth-century newspaper publisher Joseph Pulitzer and were established in 1917. Pulitzer left a bequest to Columbia University for the prizes, and the university has administered them ever since. The Pulitzer Center, or more formally, the Pulitzer Center for Crisis Reporting, was founded in 2006 with the goal of raising the quality of reporting on international crises. Sometime later, it made "educational outreach" part of its "core mission." The outreach it had in mind was teaching aspiring journalists to see themselves as "engaged global citizens."

"Global citizens" is a widely used phrase on the campus left. It signals disenchantment with the idea of the nation-state and with "citizenship" as usually understood. Global citizens are, at least by disposition, loyal to no particular place, people, culture, or government. They are "post-national" and see themselves as operating on a plane above the parochial attachments of ordinary people. Global citizenship is a self-conferred elite status, but it helps to have a peer group of similarly liberated intellectuals and some sponsoring organizations that are willing to write checks to support expressions of the attitude.

In choosing the Pulitzer Center, the *New York Times* picked an apt partner for the 1619 Project. And the Pulitzer Center went all-in. For example, on September 27, 2019, the Pulitzer Center hosted a reception for journalists in Austin, Texas, "to exchange ideas for using journalism in classrooms to cultivate the next generation of engaged global citizens." How would these engaged global citizens be helped? "On hand will be award-winning *New York Times* journalist Nikole Hannah-Jones and Sam Dolnick, a *New York Times* assistant managing editor and Pulitzer Center board member." The Pulitzer Center's website explained that the participants could "learn about Pulitzer Center–developed educational resources for *The New York Times*' 1619 project on the legacy of slavery and racism, and *The Weekly*, the newspaper's recently launched television series."[18]

Dolnick is a frequent contributor to the *Times*, but he was not a contributor to the Sunday magazine's 1619 Project issue. What stands out in the announcement is that he is a bridge between the editorial staff of the *Times* and the board of the Pulitzer Center. The rising global-citizen journalists could indeed learn something about how the pieces fit together. The center's website lists other Pulitzer Center figures who attended the reception: Indira Lakshmanan, former executive editor at the Pulitzer Center; Steve Sapienza, a Pulitzer staff member who has produced news and documentary stories; and most importantly, Fareed Mostoufi, who is "part of the education team at the Pulitzer Center, where he focuses on designing classroom resources and connecting journalists to students." Mostoufi shows up frequently in Pulitzer Center posts about 1619 outreach efforts. He was, for example, in Winston-Salem, North Carolina, on October 10, 2019, describing to teachers "the Center's online curricula."[19]

In December 2019, the Pulitzer Center website provided an account of its "education programming," including 1619 events. At that point the center was claiming that "teachers across all 50 states have accessed the Pulitzer Center educational resources since the project's launch." We don't have a list of the schools in which these teachers work, but the website acknowledged that "educators from hundreds of schools and administrators from six school districts have also reached out to the Center for class sets of the magazine."[20]

The hub of the Pulitzer Center's assistance with the 1619 Project is a webpage where teachers can summon help with:

March 2020

All this is ample evidence of how deeply involved the Pulitzer Center has become with the 1619 Project. But the question lingers: Why has the Pulitzer Center, with its focus on international crises, chosen to enmesh itself with the *Times'* undertaking?

The closest we have to an answer is an essay by Mark Schulte, who directs the center's K-12 program. He explains that the *Times* approached the center during the summer of 2019 "with an incredible project." The *Times* was

> *looking for an education partner to bring this issue to students in far greater numbers than usual. We had worked with them before on issues related to the Arab Spring and climate change,*

but this was different. They aimed to print hundreds of thousands of extra copies for free distribution, and were committed to an outreach campaign that would spark a national conversation about the under-reported story of the legacy of slavery in the United States.

Shulte explains that this fit with the Pulitzer's focus on "big issues" and their knowledge that "slavery is not well taught." The Pulitzer Center "anticipated strong demand among educators for a reframing of this essential part of our national identity." To that end it developed "a curricular strategy, writing a full lesson plan for the framing piece by Nikole Hannah-Jones, a reading guide to the other works in the issue, an index of historical terms referenced, and a list of suggested student activities."[22]

It worked:

Dr. Janice Jackson, CEO of Chicago Public Schools, embraced the adoption of The 1619 Project and our curriculum district-wide, saying in a September blog post: "It is my sincere hope that parents and families explore the project with their children; teachers examine these curricular materials and share it with their students; and principals support staff and students as they tackle this subject."

School districts in Buffalo, Washington, DC, and Winston-Salem, NC were also early adopters of the project and curriculum, and more are picking it up as word spreads.[23]

How far beyond those districts the Pulitzer version of the 1619 Project curriculum has spread is hard to know. To date, the Pulitzer Center isn't saying. That may well be because it knows that people like me are curious.

THE SOUTHERN POVERTY LAW CENTER

The SPLC is best known for maintaining a list of "hate groups." Some of them are obvious offenders such as the Ku Klux Klan. But other groups end up on the list when the SPLC indulges in smears against the reputations of mainstream right-of-center organizations. The SPLC's own reputation has suffered as a result, and it hasn't helped the organization that it has been mired in financial and legal scandals. This might have contributed to the *Times'* choosing to partner with the untarnished Pulitzer Center, despite its lack of previous involvement with the issues of the 1619 Project. The SPLC, in fact, had a long-standing commitment to pushing a radical racial history curriculum in the schools. It even beat the *Times* to the conceit of declaring that 2019 was the 400th anniversary of slavery in America.

In January 2018, the SPLC released "Teaching Hard History: American Slavery," a report that is part of its Teaching Tolerance program.[24] The webpage presenting the report proclaims:

> *Schools are not adequately teaching the history of American slavery, educators are not sufficiently prepared to teach it, textbooks do not have enough material about it, and – as a result – students lack a basic knowledge of the important role it played in shaping the United States and the impact it continues to have on race relations in America.*[25]

The SPLC describes Teaching Tolerance as a program that "developed a framework and a set of recommendations for teaching about American slavery for students in grades 6–12."[26] The program includes an account of the

White Lion arriving at Jamestown, with its cargo of slaves, in August 1619.

But the SPLC didn't complain or assert its sense of priority when the *Times* published its 1619 Project special magazine issue. Rather, it cited and linked to Hannah-Jones's article as further evidence for the point it had long been making. The Family Research Council, which is a harsh critic of the SPLC in general and of its Teaching Tolerance program in particular, also noted that the SPLC had been way ahead of the 1619 Project. The *Times'* project, said the Family Research Council, is "just the latest version of offensive ideology and distortive historical revisionism to enter mainstream consciousness." The SPLC's Teaching Tolerance curriculum "has been saying the same things unchecked to a much larger audience for decades." The Family Research Council even concludes that Teaching Tolerance "is far more worthy of critical review and sustained attention than The 1619 Project."[27]

Maybe so, but the 1619 Project has the cultural cachet of the *New York Times*, a very adroit publicity campaign behind it, and some effective slogans. The SPLC seems to have allied itself to the 1619 Project without any difficulty at all, and through its own channels may well be incorporating 1619 Project materials into classrooms about which the Pulitzer Center knows nothing.

This by no means exhausts the list of defenders, promoters, and admirers of the 1619 Project. I have taken note of only some of the entrenched institutional defenders. In subsequent chapters, I bring in some individual polemicists who have contributed such articles as "The Shameful Final Grievance of the Declaration of Independence," "Slavery, and American Racism, Were Born in Genocide," and the artfully titled, "Slavery: Divinely Inspired and Medically Approved."

If one measure of a political project's success is its ability to incite a passionate sense of injustice, the *Times* has succeeded.

MARCH 1621

WHAT SAVED THE PILGRIMS is well known yet still astonishing. One day – March 16, 1621 – a Wampanoag chief walked into their settlement and said in English, "Welcome! Welcome Englishmen!" Events unfolded rapidly in the Pilgrims' favor in the weeks and months that followed.

A book titled *1620* and aiming to make a case that the Mayflower Compact is a better starting place for American history than the arrival of the *White Lion* near Point Comfort, Virginia, ought to have a little more to say about the Pilgrims. So I interrupt these observations and strictures about the *Times'* 1619 Project to explain what happened to that desperate group of men and women who landed on these shores in November 1620.

IDEALS

The signers of the Mayflower Compact as well as the other *Mayflower* passengers and crew suffered terribly during the winter of 1620–21, and their troubles did not end there. The *Mayflower* departed from Plymouth on April 5, taking the seventeen surviving crewmen (out of the thirty-five who landed) with it, and leaving the weak and struggling community to fend for itself. The Compact can by no stretch be taken as securing that community from famine, disease, attack from hostile Indians, or disagreements among the survivors. It seems fair to ask in light of what followed its signing, Did it do any practical good at all?

That question resembles the one that Hannah-Jones and other critics of the Founders raise about the Declaration of Independence. The parchment document declares, "We hold these truths to be self-evident, that all men are created equal, that they are endowed by their Creator with certain unalienable Rights, that among these are Life, Liberty and the Pursuit of Happiness." The Declaration, of course, did not free the 20 percent of the population held in bondage. It did, however, plant the seeds of emancipation. Statements of principle are seldom if ever carried immediately to their fullest application. We might not even bother making declarations of principle if they were that easily realized. To say "all men are created equal" is to tacitly acknowledge that, right now, they look pretty unequal, but we can hope for some improvement. The Declaration, however, did have real short-term consequences. It established the sovereignty and collective political freedom of a people. It gave purpose and direction to the war for independence that had already begun. It voiced a new national identity – and a new *kind* of national identity.

Pronouncements such as the Mayflower Compact and the Declaration of Independence are aspirational. They enunciate a simplified and pure vision of how things will be, not a description of how things are. Often this is projected onto the recent past. The Mayflower Compact's opening – "Having undertaken, for the Glory of God, and advancements of the Christian faith, and the honor of our King and Country, a voyage to plant the first colony in the Northern parts of Virginia ..." – departs from literal truth. Some of the signatories undertook the voyage "for the Glory of God." But some surely did not: They signed on as a commercial proposition or because they were bound to their masters as servants. Others may have undertaken the voyage partly for the Glory of God but also for the hope of religious freedom or simply for the sake of their families.

But "for the Glory of God" is not a misrepresentation or a lie. Saying "for the Glory of God" is itself an act of piety that has some steadying force. It says that, whatever your personal doubts or venial motives might have been when you first considered this voyage, you committed yourself to serving a godly purpose when you set foot on the ship. You weren't deceived about the collective goal of the voyage: the advancement of the Christian faith, the honor of king and country – all of it. Now you find yourself in a situation where that commitment will demand something from you more than passive assent.

Oaths, pledges, and promises all work like this. They clear away the clutter of mixed motives and temporizing and present us with a distilled truth. The cynic or worldly sophisticate can always point out that this truth is only a pretense, a "truth," whose hollowness is denoted by scare quotes, and not a reality. But such insistence on seeing only trees and no forest is itself a kind of blindness. The force of gravity acting on an object can be offset by thrust, air pressure, and wind, but gravity is still real. Trying to account for everything at once doesn't clarify anything at all. What we want from a Mayflower Compact or a Declaration of Independence is gravity, the force that keeps us rooted.

March 1621

GOVERNMENT

The settlers at Plymouth understood that they were operating to some degree outside English law. They had no
grant to the land or a charter for their settlement.[1] They
had no right under English law to establish self-government. They understood that this put them in legal peril,
and for many years afterward they sought unsuccessfully
to get a "land patent" from the British government –
though they did get legal status of a sort from the Council for New England, which King James established in
1621. In the meantime they improvised and, under the
terms of the Mayflower Compact, created a local government of their own – one strikingly different from
those of other colonies or communities in England. The
Plymouth government elected its own leaders and pretty
much required all adult men to vote. According to the
historian Eugene Stratton in *Plymouth Colony, Its History &
People, 1620–1691*:

> *With the Mayflower Compact, the colonists agreed to a form
> of democracy that would not be practiced in their homeland
> for several centuries. Though Bradford and his supporters
> had envisioned something close to a church-state, the large
> non-Separatist population prevented the full implementation
> of this idea as it was subsequently practiced in the adjoining
> Massachusetts Bay Colony. As a result, Plymouth obtained
> a reputation for having a less rigid and more moderate gov-
> ernment, though it never practiced the toleration soon to come
> to Rhode Island. Its land policy of making grants to the
> many prevented it from becoming a manorial or proprietary
> colony, such as Virginia or other English colonies would later
> become. It became something unique.[2]*

Chapter Seven

The government that Plymouth put in place was naturally small-scale but it was not informal. Adult males voted, served as grand jurymen and trial jurors, and participated in town meetings, "made virtually obligatory by assessing fines for absence."[3]

The government was devised by William Bradford, one of the authors of the Mayflower Compact, and Plymouth's governor for thirty years. "He developed Plymouth's legal code; negotiated a deal with the stock company to settle the colonists' debts for £1,800; put down the nearby Merriemount colony of libertines with armed force, and built a lucrative trade for the colony in furs, fish, and timber."[4] He did this while maintaining a high degree of religious tolerance and a commitment to private agriculture. Bradford also wrote the complete record we have of the founding of the colony, *Of Plymouth Plantation*. He explained that what prompted the Mayflower Compact was seeing the need for

> the first foundation of their govermente in this place; occasioned partly by the discontented and mutinous speeches that some of the strangers amongst them had let fall from them in the ship-That when they came a shore they would use their owne libertie; for none had power to command them, the patente they had being for Virginia, and not for New-england, which belonged to an other Goverment, with which the Virginia Company had nothing to doe. And partly that shuch an acte by them done (this their condition considered) might be as firme as any patent, and in some respects more sure.

Bradford also described what immediately followed the signing of the Compact:

After this they chose, or rather confirmed, Mr. John Carver (a man godly and well approved amongst them) their Governour for that year. And after they had provided a place for their goods, or common store, (which were long in unlading for want of boats, foulnes of winter weather, and sicknes of diverce,) and begune some small cottages for their habitation, as time would admitte, they mette and consulted of lawes and orders, both for their civill and military Govermente, as the necessitie of their condition did require, still adding therunto as urgent occasion in severall times, and as cases did require.[5]

What exactly these "laws and orders" were, Bradford doesn't say, but the new government considered them binding on the whole company of 102 men, women, and children, not just the forty-one members of the religious congregation.

SAMOSET

We know quite a lot about what happened after the passengers of the *Mayflower* disembarked. The Pilgrims kept good records, and historians have spent countless hours poring over them, crafting compelling accounts of life in the colony during the early years. Scholars have also traced the settlers back to their lives and families in England and the Netherlands. We could hardly hope for a more vivid picture of a marginal English settlement on the edge of the known world.

The Pilgrims' determination to govern themselves by law enabled their survival. But the great fortuitous event was when Samoset, a Native American, walked up to them and greeted them in English. Samoset had learned some English from English fishermen, who had been venturing into the coastal waters of New England for a generation to fish as well as to trade with the Indians. It was no accident that Samoset appeared, and it was not just his own curiosity that brought him to the Pilgrims. He was sent by Massasoit, the sachem (elected chief) of the Wampanoag confederation. Massasoit was weighing his difficult choices. An epidemic disease had taken a devastating toll on his people, and he feared that his hostile neighbors to the west, the Narragansetts, would overrun his tribe. He sent Samoset to begin to explore the idea that the Plymouth settlers could be his allies against the Narragansetts.

The first contact with the Plymouth settlers went well. Samoset provided detailed descriptions of the country where the Pilgrims had landed and its inhabitants. He stayed the night and returned the next day with five men, whom the Pilgrims entertained. They also stayed. Then on March 22, Samoset introduced another Indian, Tisquantum (also known as Squanto), who spoke fluent English, having been enslaved once by an Englishman and having spent several years in England. Tisquantum carried the conversation forward to the point where Massasoit himself ventured forth to meet the settlers. Edward Winslow and Stephen Hopkins, guided by Tisquantum, paid a return visit to Massasoit, and negotiations proceeded.

The Pilgrims survived, just as the schoolbooks for generations have said, because the Indians taught them how to live in their new landscape, but also because the Pilgrims fell into a useful place in the complicated chessboard of alliances and hostilities among half a dozen Native American tribes. Mutually beneficial misunderstandings added to recognition of common interests.

Neither side quite knew what the other wanted, but they contrived to get along, and the alliance lasted for twenty-five years.

Others have told this story deftly and with depth of detail.[6] I simply want to underscore that when Plymouth Colony was faced with a great likelihood of failure, it somehow found the capacity to act in a coordinated and trustworthy manner. It sought to make up for past transgressions that members of the Plymouth community had committed; it avoided violence; it treated visitors respectfully; and it went a fair distance toward living up to those "just and equal laws, ordinances, acts, constitutions, and offices" that it had agreed to uphold in the Mayflower Compact.

Things were far from perfect, but America was catching a first glimpse of itself.

CHAPTER EIGHT

APRIL 1861

WHEN SOUTH CAROLINIANS fired the first shots of the Civil War, on April 12, 1861, at Fort Sumter in Charleston Bay, they imagined that the South held the upper hand in any ensuing conflict with the Northern states. That was because the South was the world's primary producer of cotton, the raw material for the textile industry in both England and the Northern states. Cotton, as Southerners saw it, was an indispensable good that no one else could supply in quantity, and they wrongly believed its production undergirded the entire economy of America – and of the United Kingdom, then the world's leading industrial power.

This proved to be a fatal miscalculation. The Union blockade of Southern ports was not foolproof, but it was sufficient to persuade the British to encourage cotton production in Egypt and India. Moreover, the industrial economy of the North proved far less reliant on the agricultural economy of the South than the bellicose Southerners had supposed.

Plantation-based production of cotton in the South depended on slave labor. This gave the South a strong motive to defend slavery, and it tied slavery to the idea – the theory – that "Cotton is King." That was the idea that the fundamental wealth of America was bound to this single crop.

The South's defeat in the Civil War put an end to the King Cotton conception of the American economy. Or so it seemed for about 150 years. But in the 2010s, the idea was suddenly reborn among a handful of historians who are known for their contributions to what is called the "new history of capitalism," sometimes referred to as NHC. The three principal contributors to NHC are Walter Johnson, in his book *River of Darkness: Slavery and Empire in the Cotton Kingdom*; Sven Beckert, in his book *Empire of Cotton: A Global History*; and Edward E. Baptist, in his book *The Half Has Never Been Told: Slavery and the Making of American Capitalism*.[1] These are major works of history, rich in detail and very well written. Baptist's book is also replete with tables of statistics (e.g., "Net Internal Forced Migration by Decade," for Alabama, Arkansas, Florida, Georgia, Kentucky, Louisiana, Mississippi, Missouri, South Carolina, Tennessee, and Texas).[2] Those who want to explore still further the realm of NHC speculation should consult *Slavery's Capitalism: A New History of American Economic Development*, edited by Beckert and Seth Rockman, which compiles essays by fourteen scholars intent on restoring King Cotton to the throne.[3]

The basic idea in the books by Johnson, Beckert, and Baptist is that production of cotton in the South, inextricably linked to slave labor, formed the real basis of American prosperity in the nineteenth century. The three historians emphasize different parts of the story. Johnson pays particular attention to the Mississippi Valley. Beckert's "global history" is exactly that, with particular attention to the role played by England. Baptist addresses slavery across the South as the foundation of capitalism, and emphasizes that this form of capitalism involved constant intensification of torture to force slaves to higher levels of production.

Slavery undoubtedly brought concentrated wealth to the South. Johnson notes that "by 1860, there were more millionaires per capita in the Mississippi Valley than anywhere else in the United States." (Remember that sentence.) That was because land was relatively cheap, slave labor was abundant, river transportation by steamboat was efficient, and European demand for cotton was unrelenting. The only limiting factor was political. Johnson speaks of the "tension between the promiscuity of capital and the limits prescribed by the territorial sovereignty of the United States." He resurrects some statistical claims from antebellum Southern advocates of slavery (e.g., "the South provided two-thirds of the nation's exports"). But Southerners also noted that, because of tariffs, much of Southern wealth was transformed "into a subsidy to Northern manufacturers." Nor was this wealth exclusively in the form of cotton exports. The Mississippi Valley hosted a lively commerce in

> *flour and corn harvested from the fields of Missouri, Kansas, and Illinois; salted beef, pork and lard from animals raised and slaughtered a thousand miles away; hides and furs from Michigan, Wisconsin, and Minnesota; cattle, hogs, horses, and mules from an animal economy that stretched into the far regions of the West; "Old Monongahela" whiskey from distilleries along the Ohio, and tobacco from Kentucky.*

The "steamboat economy" grew apace, so much so that by the mid-1840s, steamboats serviced every navigable waterway along the Father of Waters and the steamboat industry had become highly competitive. All of this economic activity, of course, was facilitated by slave labor.[4]

The books by Johnson, Beckert, and Baptist deserve the considerable attention they have received, and I would give them still more, if that didn't pull this book away from its subject: the 1619 Project. But to say these books are worth reading is not to say that they are accurate or that they have persuaded everyone. They have not persuaded economists and economic historians outside the new-history-of-capitalism circle. For example, a pair of economists, Alan Olmstead and Paul Rhode, state in the abstract for their 2018 essay "Cotton, Slavery, and the New History of Capitalism": "All three authors mishandle historical evidence and mis-characterize important events in ways that affect their major interpretations on the nature of slavery, the workings of plantations, the importance of cotton and slavery in the broader economy, and the sources of the Industrial Revolution and world development."[5] If so, that doesn't leave much of their work standing.

DESMOND'S THESIS

That these works of the new history of capitalism might not be *sound* history bears on the 1619 Project because the new King Cotton thesis was incorporated in the second major essay in the August 18, 2019, issue of *The New York Times Magazine*. The essay by Matthew Desmond is titled "In Order to Understand the Brutality of American Capitalism, You Have to Start on the Plantation."

Desmond is a sociology professor at Princeton whose works include *Race in America* (2015), which is an undergraduate textbook coauthored with Mustafa Emirbayer; *The Racial Order* (2015), in which Emirbayer is first author; and *Evicted: Poverty and Profit in the American City* (2016), which won a Pulitzer Prize and has become assigned reading at many colleges. He is also, like Nikole Hannah-Jones, a recipient of the MacArthur Foundation's "genius" fellowship. *Evicted* focuses on poverty in Milwaukee by telling the stories of eight families with very little financial means struggling to provide themselves with rental housing. Desmond's conclusion is that these families are kept in poverty in large part because of their exploitation by landlords who grow rich by charging far too much and keeping their tenants in chronic debt.

In his contribution to the 1619 Project, Desmond attempts to link the arguments of NHC historians to the thesis that America is to this day an extraordinarily oppressive society. Early in his essay, he aligns himself with the Johnson–Beckert–Baptist revival of the King Cotton idea:

> *Slavery was undeniably a font of phenomenal wealth. By the eve of the Civil War, the Mississippi Valley was home to more millionaires per capita than anywhere else in the United States. Cotton grown and picked by enslaved workers was the nation's most valuable export. The combined value of enslaved people exceeded that of all the railroads and factories in the nation. New Orleans boasted a denser concentration of banking capital than New York City. What made the cotton economy boom in the United States, and not in all the other far-flung parts of the world with climates and soil suitable to the crop, was our nation's unflinching willingness to use violence on nonwhite people and to exert its will on seemingly endless supplies of land and labor. Given the choice between modernity and barbarism, prosperity and poverty, lawfulness and cruelty, democracy and totalitarianism, America chose all of the above.*[6]

He has a great deal more to say about the cruelties inflicted on slaves and the barbarity of the slave system, but Desmond never loses sight of his target: America's particularly despicable form of capitalism.

In Desmond's view, not all capitalist societies are equally bad. Some protect workers' rights via trade unions: he cites Italy and Canada. Some take care of temporary workers: he cites Brazil and Thailand. Some guard workers against abrupt dismissals: he cites Indonesia and Portugal. America, however, rates at or the near the bottom on every scale. That's because we practice what he calls "low-road capitalism" – that is, a form of capitalism that oppresses workers because of its focus on competition over prices rather than on competition over the quality of goods. To keep prices low, businesses pay workers as little as possible.

As Desmond pieces things together, the United States embarked on this low road during the era of cotton plantations: "That culture would drive cotton production up to the Civil War, and it has been a defining characteristic of American capitalism ever since." In this fashion, Desmond joins forces with Hannah-Jones to enunciate a new form of American exceptionalism in which the United States is uniquely awful. For Hannah-Jones, our exceptionalism is that we elevated the concept of freedom but then denied freedom to the slaves and provided only impaired freedom to the descendants of slaves. Slavery itself is bad, but it is much worse, according to Hannah-Jones, in a society that pretends to recognize human dignity. For Desmond, our exceptionalism is that we perfected a way of "acquiring wealth without work" by "abusing the powerless." We created a culture of "staggering inequality and undignified working conditions."

Our capitalism is "a racist capitalism" that "didn't just deny black freedom but built white fortunes."[7]

To fill in this argument, Desmond draws lots of parallels between plantations and contemporary businesses, and between the slave economy and modern financial markets. "Cotton was to the 19th century what oil was to the 20th: among the world's most widely traded commodities." Today's companies "record and analyze" evidence of workers' productivity; so too did the plantations. Modern companies depreciate assets; plantations depreciated slaves as they grew older. Modern companies "capitalize on economies of scale"; likewise, plantations. Every modern enterprise keeps meticulous books; "plantation entrepreneurs developed spreadsheets." Modern companies keep track of capital equipment; plantations kept tabs on "axes and other potential weapons."[8]

This kind of thing goes on: "The cotton plantation was America's first big business, and the nation's first corporate Big Brother was the overseer." The American corporation presents "complicated workplace hierarchies"; the antebellum plantation pioneered the idea. America today has been through some forty years of "financialization of its economy"; Desmond finds that the roots of this extend back before 1980, when Congress repealed many of the 1933 banking regulations, and back before the 1944 Bretton Woods agreement. Its roots, he says, are to be found in slavery, with "enslaved people ... used as collateral for mortgages." Desmond likens these mortgages to the "collateralized debt obligations (C.D.O.s), those ticking time bombs backed by inflated home prices in the 2000s. C.D.O.s were the grandchildren of mortgage-backed securities based on the inflated value of enslaved people sold in the 1820s and 1830s." Like CDOs, mortgaged slaves became a factor in "global financial markets," and those markets, like our instruments based in phony subprime mortgage loans, eventually collapsed.[9]

Desmond provides shout-outs along the way to John-son, Beckert, Baptist, and several other NHC scholars. He quotes Beckert and Seth Rockman's claim that "American slavery is necessarily imprinted on the DNA of American capitalism." He quotes Baptist on the use of slaves to securitize debts as amounting to "a new moment in international capitalism, where you are see-ing the development of a globalized financial market." And he quotes Johnson on the environmental degrada-tion that always follows in capitalism's footsteps, which "rendered one of the richest agricultural regions of the earth dependent on upriver trade for food."[10]

Desmond's synthesis of anticapitalism and the thesis that slavery is at the heart of everything bad in America is presented eloquently and persuasively. If you know nothing else about the time and place, and very little about economics, it would probably win your assent. It is by a large measure the most intellectually cogent essay among the thirty-four pieces of various sorts printed in the 1619 Project magazine issue.

MARKET ECONOMISTS (AND OTHERS) RESPOND

Desmond's essay is second only to Hannah-Jones's in attracting the attention of historians and other scholars, much of it severely critical. The figure who stands out as Desmond's most trenchant critic is Phillip W. Magness, a fellow of the American Institute for Economic Research. I will save him for last, after taking a tour of the points made by some of the other critics.

Chapter Eight

W. B. Allen, a professor of political philosophy and dean of James Madison College at Michigan State University, doesn't mention Desmond by name but goes straight to the central idea that American economic success is "the result of the labors of enslaved persons and thus, the system of slavery." Allen tartly points out that this amounts to a "utilitarian apology for slavery," since it means slavery ultimately produced "the greatest good for the greatest number."[11] That is, America became an immensely prosperous society, with wealth spread further than in any previous human society. Desmond meant nothing of the kind, of course, but he, like Hannah-Jones, has painted himself into a corner. Desmond's efforts to get out of that corner depend on his convincing us that America is not prosperous but rather miserable, stuck in its "low-road capitalism." This gives the reader the choice of believing his own eyes as he looks at our apparent prosperity, or joining Desmond, whose eyes are locked on trailer parks in the slums on the outskirts of Milwaukee.[12]

Allen chastises those (like Desmond) who push the slavery-begat-capitalism thesis by pointing out that "to discount the value of free labor ... in ... comparison with slave labor ... creates a false impression of relatively greater wealth in the slave economy." Some slaveholders were indeed rich, but the slave-based society they created "was decidedly less wealthy" than the free parts of America. He also observes that "none of the great industrial, transportation, communications and innovative advances in the United States derived from the outputs generated by slavery."[13]

Let me translate this. The Southern aristocracy lounged in ill-gotten wealth and did nothing to advance basic infrastructure, industry, or invention. Slavery bred decadence among the slave owners and imposed misery on everyone else. This makes it a little harder to credit the Johnson–Beckert–Baptist idea that slavery was the beating heart of American capitalism. Capitalism is a dynamic system that drives innovation. Slavery is essentially static. Even when it is hell-bent on its own expansion, slavery only reproduces itself. The expansion of slavery in the South produced more cotton and yet more slavery. The North produced cities, factories, infrastructure, and a tide of industrial invention.

Allen's critique of the economics of slavery does not stand uncontested. For example, Robert Paquette, emeritus professor of history at Hamilton College, observes:

> *The antebellum South had one of the highest rates of economic growth in the world at that time. Yes, it trailed the North, but the economic critique of slavery is better centered on the idea of sustainable growth or economic development, especially given its impact on the development of human capital and its retardation of internal markets. There is also the argument as to whether profit-consciousness and market-responsiveness constitutes capitalism in the first place. Marx would not have thought so. Nor would have Schumpeter. In the antebellum South, the majority of slaveholding units were ten or less. Market forces were concentrating slaves in fewer hands by 1860. Whereas one-third of adult white males owned slaves in 1850, only one-quarter did in 1860.*[14]

For Harris, Southern slavery impoverished the surrounding society; for Paquette, slavery retarded economic development. Neither scholar accepts the idea that the antebellum economy centered on slavery was a form of capitalism.

Recognition that the institution of slavery impoverishes a society goes back at least as far as Tocqueville.

Chapter Eight

One of the famous passages in *Democracy in America* (1835) describes "differences between the right and left banks of the Ohio." Tocqueville contrasts the settlements he sees on the right bank of the Ohio River as he travels downstream, where he sees the free state of Ohio, with those on the left bank, where he sees the slave state of Kentucky:

> [*The traveler*] *steering a path between freedom and slavery, so to speak, . . . has only to look about him to judge immediately which is the more beneficial for mankind.*
>
> *On the left bank of the river the population is sparse; occasionally a group of slaves can be seen loitering in half-deserted fields; the primeval forest grows back again everywhere; society seems to be asleep; man looks idle while nature looks active and alive.*
>
> *On the right bank, by contrast, a confused hum announces from a long way off the presence of industrial activity; the fields are covered by abundant harvests; elegant dwellings proclaim the taste and industry of the workers; in every direction there is evidence of comfort; men appear wealthy and content: they are at work.*

Tocqueville draws out this contrast still further and attributes it to the difference between slavery and freedom. In Kentucky, "work is connected with the idea of slavery," while in Ohio, work is connected "to the idea of prosperity and progress." Slavery demotivates even the nonslave, since working is a badge of "humiliation." And slavery corrupts "the very soul" of the master too: "Living in relaxed idleness, he has the tastes of idle men; he is less interested in wealth than excitement and pleasure and he deploys in this direction all the energy his neighbor devotes to other things."[15] Tocqueville's portrait of slavery ironically does not sit well with some of those today who insist that American slavery is the root of American prosperity. Ta-Nehisi Coates, for example, finds Tocqueville's account "thin and devoid of the sort of skepticism which Tocqueville shows in admirable quantity throughout the book."[16]

This critique of slavery as economically ruinous comes up over and over again among the scholars who have peered into the NHC writings, even before Desmond's essay. Writing in August 2018, Deirdre McCloskey, emerita professor of economics, history, English, and communication at the University of Illinois, observes: "Slavery made a few Southerners rich; a few Northerners, too. But it was ingenuity and innovation that enriched Americans generally, including at last the descendants of the slaves." McCloskey nails down a few other key points against the NHC theory:

> *The enrichment of the modern world did not depend on cotton textiles. Cotton mills, true, were pioneers of some industrial techniques, techniques applied to wool and linen as well. And many other techniques, in iron making and engineering and mining and farming, had nothing to do with cotton. Britain in 1790 and the U.S. in 1860 were not nation-sized cotton mills.*

And the production of cotton, contrary to NHC historians' claims, never really depended on slave labor. Cotton could be produced economically with paid labor, as it was in India and China, and eventually in the United States. In fact, after the Civil War, "by 1870, freedmen and whites produced as much cotton as the South produced in the slave time of 1860."[17]

John Clegg, a fellow at the University of Chicago, and

a contributor to the radical-left journal *Jacobin*, joins the debate at a different point. Clegg observes that cotton was a widely traded commodity and America's principal export in the antebellum era, but he notes "that exports constituted a small share of American GDP (typically less than 10 percent) and that the total value of cotton was therefore small by comparison with the overall American economy (less than 5 percent, lower than the value of corn)." King Cotton's throne turns out to be little more than a stool by the side of the road. Clegg directly disputes some of Desmond's ancillary claims, such as the idea that the "South was a net importer of food." Most of the South's wealth was immobile, "tied up in land and slaves, such that the net effect on real accumulation was probably negative." Clegg bats down Desmond's fanciful argument that the South was "a hot-bed of dynamic innovation in finance and accounting."[18] He sees among slave owners only a willingness to imitate innovations already established elsewhere in the American economy. Clegg's arguments are especially interesting in that he himself is a tough-minded critic of American capitalism. He just finds Desmond's arguments specious.

From a contrasting philosophical perspective, William L. Anderson, a fellow of the Mises Institute and professor of economics at Frostburg State University, takes issue with Desmond's idea that what made slavery profitable in the United States was, in Desmond's words, "our nation's unflinching willingness to use violence on non-white people and to exert its will on seemingly endless supplies of land and labor." As Anderson points out, this insinuates that "slave labor was more valuable than free labor,"[19] and that violence-driven slave labor was especially valuable. But comparisons to other countries vitiate both ideas. Cotton was successfully grown elsewhere in large quantities without slaves and without violence.

The efficiency of the antebellum plantations, however, has been a perennial debate among historians, some of whom argue that plantations were highly efficient, at least in comparison to the free farms in the North. The generally accepted explanation for plantation efficiency is not the effort to drive slaves harder, but the efficiencies of scale achieved by ever-bigger plantations worked by ever-increasing crews of slaves organized in coordinated ways. Robert William Fogel's *Without Consent or Contract* (1989) provides detailed documentation of the effects of large-scale agriculture and "gang labor" during the great cotton boom of the 1850s.[20]

Anderson believes the use of slaves was motivated not by the abundance of slaves but by the scarcity of any kind of labor, "so slavery provided economic stability." Slavery did make the plantation system of production possible, but that is not to grant it any claim to general economic efficiency. In one of the most pungent criticisms collected here, Anderson writes: "To declare, as Desmond does, that slavery was super-productive and that the source of the productivity came from beatings, whippings, killings, and other atrocities is so ludicrous on its face as to make one wonder why anyone takes the New History School seriously."[21]

Hans Eicholz, a senior fellow at the Liberty Fund, rips through Desmond's depiction of the contemporary American economy before settling in on Desmond's provocative idea that plantation slavery is the origin of modern double-entry bookkeeping – where debits and credits are both entered and must match. According to Eicholz, Desmond is off by about five hundred years: it was invented in late medieval Italy and perfected by Luca

Pacioli in 1494. Businessmen all over the Western world were familiar with it before the first American plantation met the first American slave. "Plantation managers did not invent the managerial or accounting techniques employed in the North; they adopted already established practices, and those methods were in fact in deep tension with their own feudal self-image."[22]

John Phelan, an economist at the Center of the American Experiment, mocks Desmond's parallel between the whipping of slaves who failed to meet their cotton quotas and the plight of the modern office worker who is chewed out for playing "Fantasy Football on company time." Desmond's slick comparisons fall apart the moment you realize the enormity of a real whipping. Perhaps Desmond is so mesmerized by his thesis that it never occurs to him that, as Phelan observes, "this nonsense is grotesquely offensive to the victims of slavery."[23]

Phelan goes on to link Desmond's fantastical estimates of the South's cotton wealth to the wild claims of Ta-Nehisi Coates, who testified to Congress that, "by 1836 more than $600 million, almost half of the economic activity in the United States, derived directly or indirectly from the cotton produced by the million-odd slaves." Horrifying if true, but in fact "the number is completely bogus." (Phelan's refutation draws on Magness's work, which I will turn to shortly.) Two more Parthian shots from Phelan are worth noting. If Desmond is right about the prosperity of the South, "why did the Confederacy lose the Civil War?" It lost, says Phelan, because of the North's "vastly superior industrial machine." Phelan also observes, correctly I think, that Desmond's claims are part of an academic debate with serious consequences: "Congress is being lobbied to take billions of dollars from one group of Americans and give them to another group," which is "a political shakedown, pure and simple," based on "dodgy numbers."[24]

Phelan may, however, overstate his case. Paquette observes:

> *In this vibrant slave economy, the profitability of slavery was increasing, not decreasing, in the decades leading up to the Civil War. The upward trajectory of slave prices generally followed the upward trajectory of upland cotton prices. Rational planters, benefiting from the rising demand for cotton in British textile factories, paid for the rising cost of slaves by becoming more efficient producers. Without the Civil War, the profitable use of slaves may well have continued deep into the 20th century.*[25]

But with the outbreak of war and the commencement of the Union blockade of Southern ports, the market conditions turned distinctly unfavorable. Paquette reminds us, however, that slavery wasn't destined on economic terms to fade away. As a system of production it had not only survived financial setbacks and technological advances, it had gone on to prove its efficiency and durable commercial value. Its moral faults and its cultural consequences were not enough to put it on the road to extinction. That would require Lincoln's leadership and the determination of the North to preserve the union. It would also require some shrewd reckoning on the deeper economic contradictions of slavery, which produced only a certain kind of prosperity and a great deal of poverty.

MAGNESS OPUS

Phillip W. Magness had been writing in opposition to the Johnson–Beckert–Baptist interpretation of the history of capitalism for several years before the 1619 Project was launched. If there was anyone in the United States prepared to counter Desmond, it was Magness. When Coates wrote that "almost half of the economic activity in the United States derived directly or indirectly from the cotton produced by the million-odd slaves," he was relying on Baptist's major contribution to the NHC library; when Phelan challenged Coates, he was relying on Magness. Baptist had conjured the $600 million ("almost half the economic activity in the United States" in 1836) by taking the $77 million in economic activity represented by cotton production and adding other transactions in some fashion connected to cotton production. As Magness points out, this is "a fundamental accounting error." Gross domestic product (GDP) "only incorporates the value of final goods and services produced," not the costs of intermediate transactions. When Baptist throws in "things like land purchases for plantations, tools used for cotton production, transportation, insurance, and credit instruments used in each," he wildly inflates the economic value of cotton production in 1836. The trouble is that those factors such as land purchases are already included in the price of the cotton production, so Baptist has counted them twice, or, because he is counting other goods in which the price of land is also included, Baptist ends up counting some factors over and over again. Thus $77 million balloons to $600 million, and that cotton ball expands to absorb half the US economy.[26]

Magness credits several economists for catching this error when Baptist's book came out in 2014, among them Olmstead and Rhode, who observe that Baptist reached his $600 million figure "by double counting and bad national product accounting." Baptist "inexplicably adds 'the money spent by millworkers and Illinois hog farmers.'" Why stop at $600 million? As Olmstead and Rhode see it, Baptist, in counting what he called "third-order effects," could just as easily have found the economic value of cotton production to "exceed 100 percent of GDP."[27]

Olmstead and Rhode, however, do not dwell on Baptist's incompetence at accounting. Their bigger fish is his incompetence as a historian, and they expend much effort on dismantling his theory that "innovations in calibrated torture propelled southern and world development." This argument turns out to derive from a few anecdotal sources and to ignore the biggest factor in increased cotton production: the introduction of improved, higher-yield varieties of cotton. Baptist makes much of the idea of the "pushing system" whereby quotas for picking cotton were relentlessly increased. But, they write, "the 'pushing system' is Baptist's invention; there is no evidence that contemporary actors used this term or that such a system even existed." Baptist "appears to have coined the term, 'pushing system,' based on the use of the word 'pushing' by one Florida slave in a purported chance 1834 or 1835 conversation reported by Philemon Bliss, a northern abolitionist."[28]

Coates's use of Baptist's numbers in congressional testimony five years after *The Half Has Never Been Told* was published shows how the conceit wormed its way into the new slavery narrative, regardless of its inaccuracy. Magness, reviewing other refutations that were brushed aside, observes that other historians, equally baffled by basic economics, attempted to one-up Baptist. "Not to be outdone by Baptist's erroneous 50 percent estimate, Emory University historian Carol Anderson" calculated that in 1860, "80 percent of the nation's gross national product was tied to slavery."[29]

Baptist's book attracted other sharp critiques, including Paquette's 2016 review on the *Law & Liberty* site, which helpfully traces the historical debates that preceded Baptist's "deeply flawed and tendentious volume." Paquette points out that "Baptist's interpretation comes down in the vicinity of Fogel and Engerman, albeit after traipsing through suspicious corridors into fantastical precincts where the two economists would not have followed."[30] Robert Fogel and Stanley Engerman's (now classic) 1974 book *Time on the Cross* used hard economic data to show that the plantation system was profitable.[31] Fogel dug even deeper in his 1989 volume, *Without Consent or Contract.* But Baptist goes further, says Paquette, by implausibly attributing increased plantation productivity to "'the whipping-machine' to extract from beleaguered slave bodies on cotton plantations 'super-profits' that erected the United States, by 1840, into a global economic colossus."[32]

Yet another notable review of Baptist's work is Trevor Burnard's, in the journal *Slavery & Abolition*. Burnard starts out by observing that *The Half Has Never Been Told* is "badly written, sometimes spectacularly so. It is inadequately researched and shows a lack of familiarity with economic theory. It is overblown and full of overstatements. Most disturbingly," he goes on, the book is "scandalously deficient" in its citations.[33] And that's just Burnard warming up. Yet another crushing critique of Baptist's book was published by Stanley Engerman.[34]

If we seem to have wandered a bit from Desmond's contribution to the 1619 Project, we haven't really. Baptist and the other NHC historians are the foundation of everything Desmond has to offer. Johnson, Beckert, and Baptist write as if the profitability of plantation slavery is a new discovery, and they twist profitability into the claim that the plantations were "capitalist." That plantations made money, however, is one thing. Capitalism is something else. In Magness's view, the HNC historians' arguments sound very similar to "the late antebellum bluster of James Henry Hammond," who likewise exaggerated the world-historical importance of cotton: "You dare not make war on cotton – no power on earth dares make war upon it. Cotton is king."[35]

Magness, more than any other economist, has devoted his attention to tracking how the 1619 Project follows in spirit and letter the conjuring of the New Historians of Capitalism. Within a week of the publication of the 1619 Project, he published "How the 1619 Project Rehabilitates the 'King Cotton' Thesis" in *National Review*.[36] In December he published "Fact Checking the 1619 Project and Its Critics,"[37] followed in January 2020 by "The 1619 Project Debate: A Bibliography."[38] In February, he offered "The Case for Retracting Matthew Desmond's 1619 Project Essay."[39] These essays add robust detail to the account he had already given of the errors in Baptist's writings, zero in on Desmond's particular adaptation of the NHC thesis, and distill the observations of other critics. Read "The Case for Retracting" for the best summation to date of where Desmond goes astray.

One comment by Magness speaks directly to the quality of the scholarship behind the whole 1619 Project: "When I asked her about Desmond's overreliance on Ed Baptist's debunked claims, project editor Nikole Hannah-Jones responded, 'Economists dispute a few of Baptist's calculations but not the book itself nor its thesis.'" Hannah-Jones's brushing aside of a profoundly important mistake in a key source reveals more about the shaky foundations of her project than she seems to realize.

In March, Magness published another piece, hopefully titled "The 1619 Project: An Epitaph."[40] He refers

to the decision by the *Times* (which I discussed in an earlier chapter) to add the words "some of" to Hannah-
Jones's original claim that the colonists rebelled because
they feared that Britain would emancipate the slaves. Ah,
so it's only *some of* the colonials who acted on this fear.
Magness sees this as a "stunning concession," which "gave
away the game." He correctly observes that the correction is in the form of "tepid backtracking" and "guarded
conciliatory language," with no outright admission of
error. But Magness is happy to read this as the *Times'*
painful retreat after six months of "aggressive derision"
of its critics.

I will be surprised if the aggressive derision now stops.
The *Times* has done the minimum necessary to patch a
gaping hole in its credibility. As Magness notes in passing, the newspaper "has thus far evaded scrutiny of Desmond's claims."

CHAPTER NINE

JANUARY 1863

IN HER LEAD ESSAY for the 1619 Project, Nikole Hannah-Jones calls out Abraham Lincoln as a racist. Her evidence for this charge is an August 14, 1862, White House meeting between Lincoln and five black leaders in which Lincoln "informed his guests that he had gotten Congress to appropriate funds to ship black people, once freed, to another country." Lincoln said, as Hannah-Jones quotes him: "Why should they leave this country? This is, perhaps, the first question for proper consideration. You and we are different races. . . . Your race suffer very greatly, many of them, by living among us, while ours suffer from your presence. In a word, we suffer on each side."[1] He seems to call for treating whites and blacks in dramatically different ways, to the disadvantage of blacks. Lincoln did not propose deporting any European Americans back to the continent of their ancestral origins. The phrase "ours suffer from your presence" certainly sounds both insulting and racist.

But there is more to the story. The questions that hang over a lot of studies of Lincoln is whether he always meant what he said, or whether he sometimes said things out of political calculation. In this chapter I explain why Hannah-Jones's account of that White House meeting is wrong, and more broadly, why Lincoln was not a racist. But we will have to give fair-minded hearings to both sides – something that Hannah-Jones herself declined to do. I will not say that her view is eyewash from beginning to end. There are historians who basically agree with her. But the weight of evidence is against them – and her.

ENDING SLAVERY

On January 1, 1863, President Lincoln issued the Emancipation Proclamation. It announced that the slaves in the states held by the Confederacy "shall be then, thenceforth, and forever free." This promised freedom to about four million people held in bondage in the Confederate states. But for the promise to be realized, Union troops would have to win many battles and vanquish the Confederacy. Actual emancipation awaited those victories.

Moreover, the Emancipation Proclamation left slavery intact in four slave states that had not joined the Confederacy: Maryland, Missouri, Kentucky, and Delaware. Tennessee had been part of the Confederacy but was under Union control, so it too was exempted. Maryland, Missouri, and Tennessee abolished slavery during the war; Kentucky and Delaware waited until after the war concluded in 1865.

The final abolition of legal slavery in the United States came with the ratification of the Thirteenth Amendment, on December 6, 1865. That amendment, promoted by Lincoln, had been passed by the Senate on April 8, 1864, and by the House on January 31, 1865.

Lincoln had decided to issue the Emancipation Proclamation six months before he actually issued it. He delayed its release pending a significant Union military victory, which finally came at the Battle of Antietam,

September 17, 1862. A few days later, on September 22, he released a preliminary version of the Proclamation.

Lincoln had been campaigning against slavery since October 1854. Initially, he focused on stopping the spread of slavery in the territories. That was the theme of his reentry into American politics (after a five-year period during which he had gone back to working as an attorney). The passage of the Kansas-Nebraska Act in 1854 overturned the 1820 Missouri Compromise, allowing Kansas and Nebraska to enter the Union "with or without slavery, as their Constitution may prescribe at the time of their admission." The act awakened a sense of urgency in Lincoln about the spread of slavery and Congress's power to regulate it in the territories.

In October 1854 he gave two major speeches, in Springfield and Peoria, that left no doubt about his profound antipathy to slavery. His three-hour Peoria speech on October 16 is generally understood as the foundation of his subsequent public career. In it he declared:

> *Slavery is founded in the selfishness of man's nature – opposition to it, in his love of justice. These principles are an eternal antagonism; and when brought into collision so fiercely, as slavery extension brings them, shocks, and throes, and convulsions must ceaselessly follow. Repeal the Missouri compromise – repeal all compromises – repeal the declaration of independence – repeal all past history, you still can not repeal human nature. It still will be the abundance of man's heart, that slavery extension is wrong; and out of the abundance of his heart, his mouth will continue to speak.*[2]

That passage from the speech was not forgotten. In his book *Lincoln at Peoria: The Turning Point* (2008), Lewis Lehrman devotes a chapter to arguing that "Peoria

Characterizes the Lincoln Presidency." He recounts how in May 1860, Mary Livermore, who was attending the Republican National Convention, asked a Massachusetts reporter whether Lincoln was feigning his opposition to slavery in order to win votes. Lehrman quotes from Livermore's memoirs, in which she wrote that the reporter took "from his pocketbook a little fragment of newspaper, which contained this extract from his 'Peoria, Ill., speech,' made Oct. 16, 1854, and passed it to me with the simple query, 'Do you think he can back track after saying that?'"[3] The newspaper fragment contained the passage I quote above.

Can we reconcile the Lincoln who gave that speech in Peoria, who drafted the Emancipation Proclamation and led the nation to ratification of the Thirteen Amendment, with Hannah-Jones's image of Lincoln as a racist? The question we need to ask is, How does Lincoln's White House meeting with five black leaders in August 1862, in which he asked what they thought of relocating freed slaves to an overseas colony, fit with Lincoln's fervent belief in human equality?

WHAT REALLY HAPPENED

Given the significance that Hannah-Jones attributes to Lincoln's remarks on that occasion, it is useful to have a fuller record of what happened. Some of his remarks on the occasion, not quoted by Hannah-Jones, bear special attention:

But even when you cease to be slaves, you are yet far removed from being placed on an equality with the white race. You are cut off from many of the advantages which the other race enjoy. The aspiration of men is to enjoy equality with the

best when free, but on this broad continent, not a single man
of your race is made the equal of a single man of ours. Go
where you are treated the best, and the ban is still upon you.

I do not propose to discuss this, but to present it as a fact
with which we have to deal. I cannot alter it if I would. It
is a fact, about which we all think and feel alike, I and you.
We look to our condition, owing to the existence of the two
races on this continent. I need not recount to you the effects
upon white men, growing out of the institution of Slavery.
I believe in its general evil effects on the white race.[4]

In the view of many historians, Lincoln's meeting with
the delegation of black Washingtonians – Edward Thomas,
John F. Cook Jr., John T. Costin, Cornelius Clark, and
Benjamin McCoy – was among the lowest points of his
presidency. The proposal for the American black population voluntarily to leave the country en masse is not
something we can look on today with pride, but as always,
when we look closely at history, things are complicated –
in fact, a lot more complicated than they may seem.

Lincoln was far from the first to consider mass emigration for freed blacks. The entire country of Liberia
had been established to promote an African home for
ex-slaves, and more than fifteen thousand American
blacks chose to emigrate to Liberia between 1822 and
the outbreak of the Civil War. (More on this below.) Lincoln's proposal set off an active debate among both white
abolitionists and leaders of the free black community.
Edward Thomas, the leader of the delegation, supported
Lincoln's proposal, and "hundreds of black Washingtonians volunteered for the first voyage." (Whereas earlier
attempts to resettle freed slaves focused on Liberia, Lincoln's 1862 proposal focused on a small island near Haiti,
and some 450 ex-slaves actually moved there. But Lincoln

Chapter Nine

soon abandoned the idea.) Thomas was a figure of note: "well-known among African Americans as an intellectual and cultural leader," active in "Israel Lyceum, one of Washington's several prewar black debating societies," and "renowned for his collections of fine art, coins, and a personal library of almost six hundred volumes."[5]

Before the meeting with Lincoln, Thomas had proposed a resolution to a black organization, the Social, Civil, and Statistical Association (SCSA), opposing such relocation, but he changed his mind. He told Lincoln in a letter that he and the others had come to the meeting "entirely hostile" to the idea but that Lincoln had won them over. It appears Thomas exaggerated. Some of the delegates remained opposed, and a strong debate continued in the black community in Washington.

This flow of events, however, does not match Hannah-Jones's reimagining of the White House meeting:

> *You can imagine the heavy silence in that room, as the weight of what the president said momentarily stole the breath of these five black men. It was 243 years to the month since the first of their ancestors had arrived on these shores, before Lincoln's family, long before most of the white people insisting that this was not their country. The Union had not entered the war to end slavery but to keep the South from splitting off, yet black men had signed up to fight. Enslaved people were fleeing their forced-labor camps, which we like to call plantations, trying to join the effort, serving as spies, sabotaging confederates, taking up arms for his cause as well as their own. And now Lincoln was blaming them for the war. "Although many men engaged on either side do not care for you one way or the other ... without the institution of slavery and the colored race as a basis, the war could not have an*

existence," the president told them. "It is better for us both,
therefore, to be separated."[6]

In fact, the members of the delegation were fully briefed
on what Lincoln would say. They had been debating the
idea for years, and Congress had begun appropriating
funds for such an enterprise in April 1862, four months
before the meeting. No one in the room was surprised by
what Lincoln said. Moreover, they were not insulted by
the idea of black emigration. Haiti as well as Africa had
been attracting free black migrants for decades. Lincoln's
proposal merely "opened a new chapter in a longstand-
ing debate among African Americans."[7]

BLUMENTHAL AND BENNETT

Whether Lincoln was a racist doesn't stand or fall on this
one meeting. Hannah-Jones finds a scattering of other
contextless quotations to buttress her idea. She writes:

> *Like many white Americans, he opposed slavery as a cruel*
> *system at odds with American ideals, but he also opposed*
> *black equality. He believed that free black people were a*
> *"troublesome presence" incompatible with a democracy*
> *intended only for white people. "Free them, and make them*
> *politically and socially our equals?" he had said four years*
> *earlier. "My own feelings will not admit of this; and if mine*
> *would, we well know that those of the great mass of white*
> *people will not."*[8]

The quotation is actually from the Lincoln-Douglas
debates.

The complications here are that Lincoln was a public

orator known for his ardent opposition to the expansion of slavery and his belief that blacks had the same fundamental rights as whites. He was frequently in a position of threading the needle: How could he advance his principles while trying to win the support of audiences who did not necessarily support, even if they did not vehemently oppose, his agenda? The lines that Hannah-Jones quotes are masterpieces of subversive rhetoric. They sound on first hearing as though Lincoln is expressing his opposition to black equality. But look again. He asks a rhetorical question and provides an equivocal answer. His *"feelings"* will not "admit" political and social equality, but as Lincoln's defenders often point out, Lincoln didn't take political and social equality off the table. He just took those topics out of the debate he was in at the moment.

Hannah-Jones's attack on Lincoln hardly went unnoticed. Amid the flood of criticisms of the 1619 Project were many that called her out for her distorted picture of the sixteenth president.

Although Hannah-Jones did not cite sources in her article, in this case her source was easily identified. Sidney Blumenthal, former aide to Hillary Clinton, has been publishing a multivolume "survey of Lincoln's political life" and writing occasional pieces on Lincoln in the *Washington Monthly*. Blumenthal took notice of Hannah-Jones's debt to Lerone Bennett Jr., an editor at *Ebony* magazine who once wrote an article called "Was Abe Lincoln a White Supremacist?" and who followed up with a book, *Forced into Glory: Abraham Lincoln's White Dream* (2000). Hannah-Jones "recapitulates Lerone Bennett's projection of Lincoln as an inveterate racist and committed white supremacist, and the Emancipation Proclamation as a sham."[9]

In a review written for none other than the *New York*

Times, the great Civil War historian and Lincoln biographer James M. McPherson immediately buried Bennett's wild accusations in the graveyard of incompetent and malicious books, describing it as "a tendentious work of scholarship, marred by selective evidence taken out of context, suppressive of contrary evidence, heedless of the cultural and political climate that constrained Lincoln's options and oblivious to Lincoln's capacity for growth."[10] Yet Bennett's incompetently researched tome was apparently a goldmine for Hannah-Jones. Bennett's writings on Lincoln have been excoriated by other scholars, including Eric Foner, who writes:

> *Bennett is not content to show that Lincoln held racist views. Racism, Bennett insists, was Lincoln's most deeply held belief, "the center and circumference of his being." The Great Emancipator, he asserts, was, in reality, "one of the major supporters of slavery in the United States" and "in and of himself, and in his objective being, an oppressor".... These statements are totally unfounded.*
>
> *Prosecutorial briefs rarely make for satisfying history. Bennett is guilty of the same kind of one-dimensional reading of Lincoln's career as the historians he criticizes.*[11]

Foner's own position is that Lincoln was indeed a racist, but he finds Bennett's characterization of Lincoln too extreme and implausible to fit the evidence.

We do get direct evidence of Hannah-Jones's reliance on Bennett's writings in an interview in a North Carolina newspaper, in which she talks of her discovery of Bennett's writings when she was a high school student and says that his work on American history set her on her current path.[12] The work that she cites in this and many similar interviews is Bennett's *Before the Mayflower.*

Chapter Nine

OAKES AND MCPHERSON

Among the historians who have picked out this particular blunder by Hannah-Jones is James Oakes, a professor of history at the Graduate Center of the City University of New York and the author of numerous books on slavery in the United States, including *Slavery and Freedom: An Interpretation of the Old South* (1990); *The Radical and the Republican: Frederick Douglass, Abraham Lincoln, and the Triumph of Antislavery Politics* (2007); *Freedom National: The Destruction of Slavery in the United States, 1861–1865* (2013); and *The Scorpion's Sting: Antislavery and the Coming of the Civil War* (2014). In an interview with Tom Mackaman for the *World Socialist Web Site*, Oakes characterizes Hannah-Jones's view of Lincoln as "ridiculous":

> *Most of what Abraham Lincoln had to say about African Americans was anti-racist, from the first major speech he gives on slavery in 1854, when he says, "If the negro is a man, why then my ancient faith teaches me that 'all men are created equal'; and that there can be no moral right in connection with one man's making a slave of another." Lincoln says, can't we stop talking about this race and that race being equal or inferior and go back to the principle that all men are created equal. And he says this so many times and in so many ways. By the late 1850s he was vehemently denouncing Stephen Douglas and his northern Democrats for their racist demagoguery, which Lincoln complained was designed to accustom the American people to the idea that slavery was the permanent, natural condition of black people. His speeches were becoming, quite literally, anti-racist.*

For a while, says Oakes, Lincoln grew "pessimistic about the possibilities of racial equality," but he "got over it."

His conversation with the black leaders in the White House "was a low point in his presidency."[13] That meeting, he notes, took place after he had drafted the Emancipation Proclamation but six months before he announced it in January 1863.

As Oakes reads that conversation, Lincoln was throwing "a sop" to white Northerners who were willing to fight to restore the Union but not to free the slaves. It is a dark time for Lincoln. The war is not going well on the battlefield and his political support is weak. Oakes points out that, in the same month he met with the black leaders, Lincoln sent his famous letter to Horace Greeley, editor of the influential *New York Tribune* and one of the founders of the Republican Party. Lincoln wrote (in part):

> *My paramount object in this struggle is to save the Union, and is not either to save or to destroy slavery. If I could save the Union without freeing any slave I would do it, and if I could save it by freeing all the slaves I would do it; and if I could save it by freeing some and leaving others alone I would also do that.*[14]

He angered abolitionists in saying this, but he had already decided on freeing the slaves in the Confederacy, so his third option was determined. The rest was rhetorical positioning. As Oakes puts it, "The only people who viewed emancipation as a military necessity were the people who hated slavery. And Lincoln was one of them."[15]

The letter to Greeley comes up again in another of Mackaman's anti-1619 Project interviews, with James McPherson. McPherson underscores that Lincoln had "already made up his mind when he wrote the letter," and had the Emancipation Proclamation ready. He adds that, in Lincoln's last speech, shortly before he was assassinated, "he came out in favor of qualified suffrage for freed slaves."[16]

CARWARDINE

Richard Carwardine, an Oxford historian who specializes in American political and religious history, is the author of "Abraham Lincoln and the Fourth Estate: The White House and the Press During the American Civil War" (the 2004 Stenton Lecture at the University of Reading); *Lincoln: A Life of Purpose and Power* (2006); and, as coeditor with Jay Sexton, *The Global Lincoln* (2011). Carwardine is another scholar interviewed by Tom Mackaman for the *World Socialist Web Site*, in a conversation devoted in large part to Lincoln's views of race and slavery. Mackaman points out that Hannah-Jones "homes in" on the White House meeting in August 1862 and the line from the Lincoln-Douglas debates in 1858. Carwardine responds by emphasizing political reality. Lincoln "knew he couldn't be elected [in 1858] if he were seen as a racial egalitarian." But Lincoln had expressed his passionate hatred for slavery since 1854. He was distinguishing between opposing slavery, which he emphatically did, and embracing equality, which he said he did not. But he was, in fact, embracing equality when he declared that the Declaration of Independence's "proposition that all men are created equal" applied "regardless of color."[17]

By the summer of 1862, Lincoln was "emotionally on edge." Carwardine says that the White House meeting was "not Lincoln's finest hour." He was "buffeted from all sides during one of the Union's lowest points of the war" and "lost the good humor that commonly lubricated his meetings with visitors." Yes, Lincoln had long been an advocate of black colonization schemes, as had been many others, white and black, since the founding in 1816 of the American Colonization Society by Robert Finley. With both private philanthropy and public support, the Society offered freed slaves the opportunity to colonize what became Liberia. About fifteen thousand American blacks chose to emigrate, and another three thousand blacks from the Caribbean. The idea of American blacks creating their own state abroad never completely vanished. It was a major part of Marcus Garvey's "Back to Africa" movement in the 1920s. But the Emancipation Proclamation "was silent on this issue." It didn't say anything about transporting freed slaves or colonization. Lincoln didn't close off the option, but he didn't pursue it after August 1862. Carwardine says that Lincoln's 1858 remark and his 1862 meeting "are real and are not to Lincoln's credit." But the 1619 Project takes them totally out of context in a way that is "historically deaf, and blind to a broader reality" that includes Lincoln's deep, mutually respectful relationship with Frederick Douglass.[18]

WILENTZ AND GUELZO

Defenders of Lincoln against Hannah-Jones's scurrilous attacks are not in short supply. Let's bring back into the discussion Sean Wilentz, the Princeton history professor and author of *The Rise of American Democracy: Jefferson to Lincoln* (2005) and, as mentioned earlier, *No Property in Man: Slavery and Antislavery at the Nation's Founding*. In addition to his criticisms of Hannah-Jones's thesis, he has much to say about her treatment of Lincoln.

In his essay "A Matter of Facts," Wilentz says Hannah-Jones's account of Lincoln "is built on partial truths and misstatements of the facts, which combine to impart a fundamentally misleading impression." He faults her for saying that Lincoln was "weighing a proclamation" to free slaves in the Confederacy when he met the black delegation in the White House. No: "Lincoln had already decided a month earlier to issue a preliminary version of the Emancipation Proclamation with no contingency of colonization, and was only awaiting a military victory, which came in September at Antietam." Moreover, Lincoln had already, in June, emancipated the slaves in Washington, DC. Wilentz emphasizes that, for Lincoln, emancipation never depended on colonization. There was no quid pro quo, as we say these days. There was only a debate among abolitionists and African Americans over which course would be better: stay in America or move overseas. Lincoln's secretary, John Hay, hated the idea of colonization as "hideous & barbarous humbug," as quoted by Wilentz, and was pleased when Lincoln "sloughed off" the idea.[19]

Hannah-Jones's failure to see the difference between Lincoln's views and those of "the white supremacists who opposed him" troubles Wilentz. For Lincoln, the phrase "all men are created equal" was "a human universal."

> [*Lincoln*] *insisted, however, that "in the right to eat the bread without the leave of anybody else, which his own hand earns,* [*the Negro*] *is my equal, and the equal of Judge Douglas, and the equal of every other man." To state flatly, as Hannah-Jones's essay does, that Lincoln "opposed black equality" is to deny the very basis of his opposition to slavery.*

Wilentz also calls out Hannah-Jones for her misuse of the phrase "troublesome presence." She wrote that Lincoln "believed that free black people were a 'troublesome presence' incompatible with a democracy intended only for white people." To the contrary, says Wilentz:

That phrase comes from an 1852 eulogy he delivered in honor of Henry Clay, describing Clay's views of colonization and free black people. Lincoln did not use those words in his 1862 meeting or on any occasion other than the eulogy. And Lincoln did not believe that the United States was "a democracy intended only for white people."[20]

Indeed it is helpful see exactly how Lincoln used the phrase "troublesome presence." Here are the relevant lines from the 1852 eulogy:

The American Colonization Society was organized in 1816. Mr. Clay, though not its projector, was one of its earliest members; and he died, as for the many preceding years he had been, its President. It was one of the most cherished objects of his direct care and consideration; and the association of his name with it has probably been its very greatest collateral support. He considered it no demerit in the society, that it tended to relieve slave-holders from the troublesome presence of the free negroes; but this was far from being its whole merit in his estimation.[21]

Hannah-Jones's attribution of this attitude to Lincoln himself is mistaken, if not dishonest. Lincoln was describing someone else's views. To whatever extent Lincoln held similar views, he did not express them in those words.

Wilentz has still more takedowns of Hannah-Jones's fast-and-loose ways with the truth, but this is perhaps enough. I should like to bury Hannah-Jones's thesis that Lincoln was a racist, but not to pile the earth so high on the grave of the idea that it becomes itself a kind of monument.

But a few more shovelfuls may be in order. Allen Guelzo, a senior research scholar in the Council of the

Humanities and director of the James Madison Program's Initiative in Politics and Statesmanship, both at Princeton, is among the most highly regarded Lincoln scholars in the world. His works include *The Crisis of the American Republic: A History of the Civil War and Reconstruction Era* (1995); "Defending Emancipation: Abraham Lincoln and the Conkling Letter, 1863," an essay printed in the scholarly journal *Civil War History* (2002); *Abraham Lincoln: Redeemer President* (1999); *Lincoln's Emancipation Proclamation: The End of Slavery in America* (2004); and *Lincoln and Douglas: The Debates That Defined America* (2008).

Guelzo is stern in his various articles pointing out errors in the 1619 Project. The title of one is "Preaching a Conspiracy Theory," and in it he writes, "the 1619 Project is not history; it is ignorance."[22] But it is in another article that Guelzo provides a crucial detail about Lincoln's White House meeting with the five black leaders. Writing that "colonization served as the great tranquilizer of white society," he suggests that the purpose of the White House meeting was to get the call for volunteer emigrants into the Washington newspapers.[23] It is good to be reminded that newspapers then, as now, could be extraordinarily gullible.

But that clue leads to this question: Who wrote the account of Lincoln's meeting with the five black leaders that Hannah-Jones and I quote? When I began looking into this, I assumed it was an official White House account written by one of Lincoln's staff members. It wasn't. Lincoln had taken the unusual step of inviting a newspaper reporter, who created a verbatim account of the meeting. Knowing that Lincoln had invited this reporter changes altogether the meaning of what Lincoln said. He was performing for a national audience, not holding a private conversation. As Lincoln biographer Michael Burlingame puts it: "Lincoln doubtless wanted the proceedings publicized to show the electorate that he was committed to colonization."[24] He used colonization as a practical means of opposing the expansion of slavery.

All of these facts are publicly available and easy to find if one goes looking. Why Hannah-Jones, a star journalist for the *New York Times*, failed to come across them in the eight months she worked on the 1619 Project leading up to its publication, and why she relied instead on the discredited writings of the conspiracy theorist Lerone Bennett or his followers, is known only to her. Why Jake Silverstein has remained steadfast in defense of Hannah-Jones's inaccurate, poorly sourced, and misleading essay is likewise known only to him.

Lincoln's reputation endured many assaults in his own time and in the century and a half since his assassination. It will survive Hannah-Jones's assault as well. But let's not underestimate the damage. Tens of thousands of schoolteachers will parrot her nonsense, and millions of American schoolchildren will read and hear it from voices that ring with authority.

COLONIZATION RECONSIDERED

Every aspect of Lincoln's public career, including his consideration of black colonization proposals, has attracted the attention of historians and other experts. The historians I have been quoting are major figures in American history, but no one would call them specialists on Lincoln's interest in sending American blacks abroad to found new colonies. There are, however, professional historians who have focused precisely on that. Here are two.

Michael Vorenberg is a professor of history at Brown University who, in his essay "Abraham Lincoln and the

Politics of Black Colonization," argues that Lincoln used "the prospect of black colonization to make emancipation more acceptable to conservatives and then abandon[ed] all efforts at colonization once he made the determined step toward emancipation in the Final Emancipation Proclamation."[25] Lincoln's first public expression of support for colonization was his 1852 eulogy for Clay, but once he started on the topic, he returned to it frequently. Twice, in 1853 and 1855, he accepted invitations from the Illinois Colonization Society to give speeches. He didn't become a leader in the movement but, to reiterate, he used it to position himself as a practical opponent of the expansion of slavery. In his debates with Stephen Douglas he brought up colonization every time Douglas tried to trap him as an outright friend to the blacks.

Lincoln as a statesman always kept his eye on his long-term objectives. What he said at any given moment was what he calculated as necessary to open new possibilities afterward. As Vorenberg points out, on the day before Lincoln issued the Emancipation Proclamation, he signed "a contract with Bernard Kock, an ambitious and unscrupulous venturer, to use federal funds to remove some five thousand black men, women, and children from the United States to a small island off the coast of Haiti."[26] This was the last time Lincoln mentioned colonization, and it was a last effort to reassure the antiblack conservatives that the end of slavery would not mean American citizenship for ex-slaves. For historians trying to take Lincoln's actions at face value, the Kock contract is another instance of confusing and contradictory behavior; but to those who see Lincoln as someone determined to realize the Declaration's promise of equality, the Kock contract is one more instance of prudent political calculation.

Vorenberg shows that the calculations behind the colonization policy are explicit in the oratory of some of Lincoln's supporters, such as Representative Francis P. Blair Jr. of Missouri. Blair said in April 1862, "We can make emancipation acceptable to the whole mass of non-slave-holders at the South by coupling it with the policy of colonization. The very prejudice of race which now makes the non-slaveholders give their aid to hold the slave in bondage will induce them to unite in a policy which will rid them of the presence of negroes."[27] The Haitian scheme soon fell apart, and its failure prompted Congress in March 1864 to withdraw any further funds for colonization.

Another scholar who dug deep into Lincoln's involvement with black colonization schemes was Phillip Shaw Paludan, who until his death in 2007 was a professor of Lincoln studies at the University of Illinois, Springfield. His essay "Lincoln and Colonization: Policy or Propaganda?" focuses on Lincoln's Second Annual Message, in December 1862, in which Lincoln argued in favor of three constitutional amendments that would together end slavery without war. Colonization was part of this approach. Paludan describes the disagreement among scholars over whether "Lincoln's advocacy of colonization was direct and honest" or "a propaganda tool" aimed at giving Lincoln space to work toward untrammeled emancipation. The latter "clears Lincoln of racial bias," while the former fuels the narrative of Lincoln the racist. "We can escape from this perplexity about Lincoln's motives toward colonization," Paludan argued, "if we consider it not as Lincoln's *plan* but as *one of* Lincoln's *plans*. Lincoln seems to have envisioned colonization as one of several things necessary to free the slaves and the nation from slavery."[28]

Chapter Nine

I myself have no claim to be a Lincoln scholar. Confronted with Hannah-Jones's disconcerting claims about our greatest president, I simply poked around a little in the available sources. It wasn't hard to find material that suggests that the story Hannah-Jones tells about Lincoln rests on flimsy foundations. Given the huge importance that the *New York Times* has assigned the 1619 Project in general and Hannah-Jones's essay in particular, one would think she or her editors would have taken care to check the validity of her key assertions. Instead, the *Times* launched the project into the rapids of historical controversy like a raft whose logs are tied together only by fraying strands of supposition and innuendo.

CHAPTER TEN

OCTOBER 1621

O N OCTOBER 3, 1863, three months after the Union victory at Gettysburg, Lincoln declared that the United States would celebrate an official Thanksgiving on November 26. Federal Thanksgiving celebrations were not a regular custom at the time. George Washington had held one in 1789, but after 1815 no president declared one until Lincoln. There was, however, a memory of an older tradition. Early modern Englishmen regularly celebrated municipal or royal thanksgivings.[1] The Pilgrims at Plymouth were known to have celebrated a three-day thanksgiving feast with the Wampanoag Indians sometime in the fall of 1620, between late September and early November.

Our knowledge of this depends on one source, a pamphlet known as *Mourt's Relation: A Journal of the Pilgrims at Plymouth* (1622). It was written by Edward Winslow and William Bradford between November 1620 and November 1621. "Mourt" referred to the London publisher George Morton. This is the description of the event in its entirety:

Our harvest being gotten in, our governor sent four men on fowling, that so we might after a more special manner rejoice together after we had gathered the fruit of our labors; they four in one day killed as much fowl, as with a little help beside, served the company almost a week, at which time amongst other recreations, we exercised our arms, many of the Indians coming amongst us, and among the rest their greatest King Massasoit, with some ninety men, whom for three days we entertained and feasted, and they went out and killed five deer, which they brought to the plantation and bestowed on our governor, and upon the captain, and others. And although it be not always so plentiful as it was at this time with us, yet by the goodness of God, we are so far from want that we often wish you partakers of our plenty.[2]

Bradford's much more detailed account of the early days of the colony, *Of Plymouth Plantation*, makes no mention of the event, though he describes the "small harvest" and colonists' satisfaction when they faced the winter "plentifully provisioned." Bradford's account, however, supplies something more important than a feast: he describes a community that is at peace and thriving inwardly. "For while some had thus been employed in affairs away from home" – exploring the area with Squanto and trading with the Indians – "others were occupied in fishing for cod, bass, and other fish, of which they caught a good quantity, every family having their portion." Wild fowl were caught in abundance, and families had so much food that "many wrote at length about their plenty to their friends in England, – not feigned but true reports."[3]

Mourt's Relation lays it on thicker:

For fish and fowl, we have great abundance; fresh cod in the summer is but coarse meat with us; our bay is full of lobsters all the summer and affordeth variety of other fish; in Septem-

ber we can take a hogshead of eels in a night, with small labor, and can dig them out of their beds all the winter; we have mussels and othus [clams or cockles] at our doors: oysters we have none near, but we can have them brought by the Indians when we will; all the spring-time the earth sendeth forth naturally very good sallet herbs: here are grapes, white and red, and very sweet and strong also. Strawberries, gooseberries, raspas, etc. Plums of three sorts, with black and red, being almost as good as a damson: abundance of roses, white, red, and damask; single, but very sweet indeed. The country wanteth only industrious men to employ, for it would grieve your hearts (if as I) you had seen so many miles together by goodly rivers uninhabited, and withal, to consider those parts of the world wherein you live to be even greatly burdened with abundance of people. These things I thought good to let you understand, being the truth of things as near as I could experimentally take knowledge of, and that you might on our behalf give God thanks who hath dealt so favorably with us.[4]

Mourt's Relation is plainly attempting to entice new colonists to this precarious settlement. "Industrious men" are needed to enjoy all those eels and sweet plums. But there lies behind the inducement a genuine spirit of delight. These are not the words of someone concocting a false story, but those of someone reveling in a dream very near to experience. "Not feigned," but a true report in the sense of being spoken from the heart.

The last sentence, referring to "the truth of things as near as I could experimentally take knowledge of," deserves special attention. The word "experimentally" stands where we would say "experiential," and it has a deep meaning in the Reformed theology of the Pilgrims. It refers to divinely implanted, salvific knowledge. The author of the letter, presumably Edward Winslow, could not make a more solemn affirmation of his fidelity to the truth.

More is to come. In early November, the Indians reported to the colonists that they had spotted a ship off of Cape Cod and thought it might be French. The Plymouth colonists, fearing that a foreign ship could be hostile, prepared by taking up arms, "whereupon every man, yea boy that could handle a gun, were ready, with full resolution that if she were an enemy, we would stand in our just defense." The ship, however, turned out to be an English vessel, the *Fortune*, which brought thirty-five new settlers "to remain and live in the plantation." *Mourt's Relation* celebrates the ship's arrival as an opportunity to prove to the world "we have not been idle, considering the smallness of our number all this summer." They load up the *Fortune* for its return trip with animal pelts – "two hogsheads of beaver and otter skins" – that they hope will persuade London merchants "to furnish us with things needful for further employment, which will also encourage us to put forth ourselves to the uttermost."[5]

The little colony, in other words, has begun to think of itself as a fledgling commercial success, and a strong "we" has emerged during that first year of privation and struggle.

Bradford's *Of Plymouth Plantation* adds some vital detail. The men aboard the *Fortune* had been disheartened by what they saw on Cape Cod. They feared starvation and attack by the Indians, and even after they landed at Plymouth, some of them "began to plot to seize the sails, lest the ship should go, and leave them there." Bradford describes most of the thirty-five newcomers as "healthy young men, many of them wild enough, who had little considered what they were undertaking."[6] These were not signers of the Mayflower Compact, but immigrants to a social order springing from that compact.

It is a test of such a social order whether it can accommodate and absorb a substantial contingent of outsiders. The captain of the *Fortune* did his part to calm their fears. He offered to take to Virginia any who wanted to leave Plymouth. This seemed to settle the restless immigrants: "So they were all landed." They arrived with no food, few clothes, and very little equipment. So, with the onset of winter, Plymouth had to absorb not just newcomers but newcomers who could not fend for themselves. Extraordinarily, "The plantation was glad of this addition of strength," even though it "wished many of them had been of better class."[7]

The *Fortune* carried with it a letter from Thomas Weston in London, who had helped outfit the *Mayflower* expedition. Weston was angry that colonists had not yet returned a financial profit for his venture, had kept the *Mayflower* at Plymouth over the previous winter, and then sent her home empty. Bradford wrote back, accepting some blame but disputing other points that Weston had presumably picked up from the ship's crew:

> *Those who told you we spent so much time in discoursing and consulting, etc., their hearts can tell their tongues they lie. They care not, so that they salve their own sores, how they wound others. Indeed it is our calamity that we are, beyond expectation, yoked with some ill-disposed people, who, while they do no good themselves, corrupt and abuse others.*[8]

This is an important clue that the "Strangers," that is, the secular Englishmen who were not part of the company of religious pilgrims, continued to trouble the little community.

Chapter Ten

Ample evidence attests to Plymouth's falling short of any utopian ideal. Like any human community, it had fractures, lawbreakers, and abundant challenges. Yet within a year of its founding and a disastrous first winter, it had emerged as a place with a highly functional division of labor that produced crops, fish, fowl, and trade goods. It had sufficient esprit de corps to send armed expeditions against hostile Indians and muster the inhabitants to defend against the chance of a French attack. It had the leadership and wisdom to negotiate a strong treaty with the Wampanoag, which would last a quarter century. It had the flexibility to absorb a substantial number of unruly young men who had no prior commitment to the community's values. It had sufficient surplus to entertain ninety Indian guests for a three-day feast. The Indians significantly outnumbered the colonists – there were only fifty left – at that first Thanksgiving, which is itself evidence of the little community's self-confidence.

Plymouth also had the confidence to rebuff an angry creditor. Above all, it had a sense of common identity, a "we" that spoke for "us."

That sense of "we" could have been merely tribal. The circumstances favored such parochialism. But Plymouth was not just that. It had the horizon that it was an English colony and it leaned on that status for English support; it saw itself as part of a New World; and it had its aspiration to be something greater. John Winthrop's famous sermon "A Model of Christian Charity," in which he pronounced that the new community would be "a city upon a hill, the eyes of all people are upon us," lay almost ten years in the future (March 31, 1630), but Bradford's writing adumbrates the idea.

A key ingredient in this emerging identity was the colony's gratitude. The relative material abundance it had gathered by October 1621 was not something it took for granted. The colonists knew full well that it could have been otherwise. They might have attributed their survival to mere good fortune, and indeed the *Fortune* did opportunely arrive. But mostly, they thanked God for his providence, and they did indeed hold a Thanksgiving celebration.

The opposites of gratitude are envy and resentment. The 1619 Project presents such feelings as righteous, justified, and to be savored as though they were delicious. Valorizing a sense of perpetual victimization can serve, like gratitude, as a social charter of sorts, but it is a charter for endless conflict and bottomless demands for reparations. In her original 1619 essay, Hannah-Jones doesn't mention reparations for slavery, but soon after, she avowed that seeking reparations was her true purpose. She says at the end of a long interview on the *Karen Hunter Show*, in December 2019, that when she was asked by her *Times* editor what her ultimate goal was, she replied, "My ultimate goal is that there will be a reparations bill passed." In fact she spends considerable time in that interview talking about other occasions on which she has advocated for reparations, and explaining what she means by reparations. Such reparations, she says, are not just for slavery but for the one hundred years after slavery, and they will have to consist of cash payments to every black American who has a slave ancestor. Their purpose will not be to erase racism, bring about racial harmony, or *fully* pay what whites owe blacks; they will simply be a form of "restitution" for what has been wrongfully taken away from blacks.[9] Hannah-Jones rehearsed this theme many times and many places, as in an interview with the *Chicago Tribune*: "If you read the whole project, I don't think you can come away from it without understanding the project is an argument for reparations. You can't read it and not understand that something is owed."[10] When she says that's her goal for the 1619 Project, she unflinchingly sticks to the logic of the emotions she has tried to put in play.

Her arguments on this culminated in another *New York Times Magazine* cover story in June 2020, "What Is Owed." To those who had followed her statements since the 1619 Project was published, the essay was unsurprising and broke no new ground. It is just a fuller declaration that blacks have been ill-treated and, in that light, should be paid a lot of money. She freely admits that such payments will do nothing to improve race relations and won't expunge any moral debt. They are simply "what is owed."[11]

There is no gratitude to be found in the 1619 Project, only bitterness and anger. It is a bucket lowered into the poisoned well of identity politics. Communities can be built in ways more gracious and yet still practical. That's the real lesson of the Mayflower Compact.

CHAPTER ELEVEN

JANUARY 2020

T HOUGH I HAVE TRACKED some of the criticisms by
professional historians of the 1619 Project, I have
left unnoted a great many contributions by historians to
the criticism and to the defense of the project. They
number too many to remark on without transforming a
short book into a long annotated bibliography.

One item in all this abundance, however, calls for special attention. In January 2020, the editor of *The American Historical Review* circulated a statement, "1619 and All
That." The statement wasn't officially published in the
journal until February 3, but by then it had been widely
read and responded to. An extract from it, with a link to
the full text, had been posted to *History News Network*, a
website hosted by George Washington University, on
January 21.[1]

The writer was Alex Lichtenstein, a professor of history at Indiana University Bloomington and the author
of *Twice the Work of Free Labor: The Political Economy of Con-
vict Labor in the New South* (1996) and coauthor of *Marked,
Unmarked, Remembered: A Geography of American Memory*
(2017).

"1619 and All That" is a comprehensive dismissal of
the criticisms by all the historians who had written to the

Times, and who had done interviews with the *World Social-ist Web Site*. It served as a kind of permission slip to thousands of other professional historians to ignore the controversy as unworthy of their time and attention. The piece provoked a furious response from the editors of the *World Socialist Web Site* as well as individual responses from some of the historians; but Lichtenstein appears to have largely succeeded in calming the great majority of historians and marginalizing the critics. He did so by deflating the debate to a "public scuffle between journalists and members of our profession" in which, he avowed, he didn't want to get involved but had to, because "it was all anyone asked me about at the American Historical Association's annual meeting during the first week of January."[2]

Lichtenstein begins his essay by mentioning that the Civil War memorial in Green-Wood Cemetery in Brooklyn makes no mention of "slavery or emancipation." It is all about preserving the Union. That observation quietly buttresses Hannah-Jones's belief that the Civil War wasn't really about slavery. He signals in this opening which side he is taking, and it is not long before he comes right out to declare that the 1619 project's "'reframing' of the country's 'origins' was a rhetorical move, one that impressed upon a wider public an interpretive framework that many historians probably already accept – namely, that slavery and racism lie at the root of 'nearly everything that has truly made America exceptional.'"[3]

He is surely right that "many historians" do accept the 1619 Project's anti-American thesis. Anyone paying attention to the history profession knows that. But Lichtenstein's casual, what's-the-big-deal attitude treats that thesis as simply what all intelligent people (within the profession) take for granted. Claiming that the "reframing" was just a "rhetorical move" also shifts the debate away from a concern about the truth. Lichtenstein continues in this carefully phrased tone of minimization: "the overall reorientation strikes me as laudable, if unexceptional."[4]

But it is not all minimization. "Many scholars initially greeted 1619 with excitement and effusive praise." In his own undergraduate teaching, he notes, he emphasizes that "the African American experience must be considered central to every aspect of American history." *Every* aspect? In any case, he finds himself "perplexed" that some historians would object to an interpretation of American history so obvious as to be anodyne.[5]

Lichtenstein continues for seven pages of this, deflecting the criticisms of the individual historians and adding reassurances of the good will embodied in the 1619 Project:

> *The lesson plans accompanying Hannah-Jones's essay, for example, emphasize the role played by the black freedom struggle in advancing democracy and liberty in America. The focus is less on the role of blacks as perpetual victims of persistent white racism than on the fact that all Americans are beneficiaries of their ceaseless fight for racial justice.*

He allows that historians may have a few valid cavils about the project but having nothing to do with its substance: "I share my colleagues' frustration that journalists occasionally draw on years of our unacknowledged research to publish under the banner of 'Extra, extra, never been told before.' But all in all, the 1619 Project is a welcome step forward."[6]

Two responses to this deserve note. First, the historian Victoria Bynum strongly objected to Lichtenstein's characterization of the critics that "all these historians are white." She observed that racial "essentialism" underlies the 1619 Project itself, as well as "much of the public reaction against historians critical of 1619."[7]

The second response is from David North and Tom Mackaman, two of the Marxists who write for the *World Socialist Web Site*. In their reply, they observe that Lichtenstein's essay "reveals the extent to which racialist mythology, which has provided the 'theoretical' foundation of middle-class identity politics, has been accepted, and even embraced, by a substantial section of the academic community as a legitimate basis for the teaching of American history." Of Lichtenstein himself, they observe that he "argues not as a conscientious historian but as a lawyer defending what he knows to be a weak case."[8]

Their language is stilted in the curious way of Marxists trying to stay within the boundaries of their intellectual commune, but their points are sharp: "A racialist narrative, which is what the 1619 Project advances, is by its very nature incompatible with empirical research and scientific methodology. It counterposes to genuine historical research a reactionary racial myth." They proceed through Lichtenstein's article point by point, demolishing as they go. (I am only sad that I cannot put the two essays side by side here.) North and Mackaman are particularly strong in defending Lincoln's motives from Lichtenstein's (and Hannah-Jones's) cynical attacks:

> *Why, one wonders, does Lichtenstein suppose the South seceded from the Union in 1861? What does he suppose Lincoln was speaking about on November 19, 1863, at the dedication of the national cemetery at Gettysburg, when he explained to a grieving nation that the meaning of the war was a "new birth of freedom"? Or in his Second Inaugural, weeks before the end of the war and his own assassination at the hands of white supremacist John Wilkes Booth, when he*

stated, "One eighth of the whole population were colored slaves, not distributed generally over the Union, but localized in the southern part of it. These slaves constituted a peculiar and powerful interest. All knew that this interest was some-how the cause of the war. To strengthen, perpetuate, and extend this interest was the object for which the insurgents would rend the Union even by war, while the Government claimed no right to do more than to restrict the territorial enlargement of it."[9]

I would leave Lincoln with the last word, but it seems important to add that we are left with a duo of hard-core Marxists to defend the integrity of American history from blasé historians, who think it no great matter that our history is being disassembled, falsified, and woven into a new fabric in the name of some sort of compensatory justice. We are fortunate that a handful of established historians came forward to defend our history, but it is deeply troubling that a figure such as Lichtenstein appears to speak for the silent majority of America's academic historians.

CHAPTER TWELVE

SEPTEMBER 2020

THE PULITZER CENTER announced its partnership with the *New York Times* in an advertisement on the inside back cover of the August 18, 2019, issue of the Sunday magazine in which the 1619 Project was launched. The text of the announcement was as follows:

THE 1619 PROJECT IN SCHOOLS

Teachers: *Looking for ways to use this issue in your classroom? You can find curriculums, guides and activities for students developed by the Pulitzer Center at pulitzercenter.org/1619. And it's all free!*

Resources include a lesson plan that introduces the issues, summaries of the articles, an index of historical terms used, suggested activities that engage students creatively and intellectually and opportunities to connect with New York Times journalists featured in this issue.

This curriculum supports students and teachers in using The 1619 Project to challenge historical narratives, redefine national memory and build a better world. — *Pulitzer Center*

Before we turn to what this means, I want to pause to consider what it looked like on the printed page.

The Pulitzer Center advertisement text was centered on the page and used the same typeface as the text of the 1619 essays themselves. It is worth taking note here that nothing in the 1619 Project conformed to the usual standards. On the cover, the reader's eye is immediately caught by the italicized capital letters accompanying lowercase roman letters. Moreover, the italicized capitals are full of swoops and curlicues, in a style that evokes some nineteenth-century script or an engraved wedding invitation. According to the website *Fonts in Use*, "an independent archive of typography," the font is a hybrid of "two custom typefaces designed for the magazine by Henrik Kubel of A2-TYPE: NYT Mag Serif and NYT Mag Sans." Unless you happen to be a specialist in typefaces, those names probably mean as little to you as they did to me. But anyone would notice that the use of italicized capital letters with lowercase roman letters looks a bit strange. It reverses a more common practice in headlines, W*here the* F*irst* L*etter* I*s* R*oman and the* R*est* A*re* I*talics*. The texts of the articles are also in a custom typeface, NYT Imperial, designed for the *New York Times*.[1]

This, of course, is a matter of style, not substance, but style contributes its mite (and its panache) to the project. It tells us that the *Times* considered the project so pathbreaking that it needed its own proprietary script. That the Pulitzer ad used the same font is an indication of how the *Times* and the organization view their partnership. The font also expresses the extraordinary status of the 1619 claims. In the essays that comprise the original magazine, in the extensive marketing of the 1619 Project since August 2019, and in the curriculum that the Pulitzer Center has helped to plant in schools, these claims seem to be lofted out of the realm of factual reportage. They are treated instead as a singular "truth," one that in the words of the magazine's editor, Jake Silverstein, "cannot be told without a clear vision of how inhuman and immoral the treatment of black Americans has been."[2] This visionary truth seems, in the judgment of the *Times*, to transcend mere facts. The special font is, in effect, the sacred script of that vision. A newspaper that styles this project as something above and beyond factual reporting is, unsurprisingly, not willing to hold its assertions to basic journalistic standards.

A DIRECT APPEAL TO TEACHERS

The Pulitzer advertisement tells us a few things even before we turn to the activities and lesson plans it heralds. First, it addresses itself to teachers – which is to say that it urges the adoption by teachers of a curriculum without the usual checks on whether that curriculum meets state and local standards. School boards are not invited to weigh in, or parents. If school administrators are to have a say, that will come later.

Teachers, of course, have considerable flexibility in setting lesson plans and organizing their classes. But a project that aims at nothing less than "to challenge historical narratives, redefine national memory and build a better world" sounds like it rises to the level where responsible bodies above the level of classroom teachers should be actively consulted. In fact, the 1619 Project calls for a "reframing" of all American history, which should be a matter of grave concern for state boards of education, governors, and legislatures.

Nothing in the Pulitzer Center's advertisement says that it or the *Times* won't pursue these higher levels of authority, but its immediate goal is plainly to persuade teachers to adopt the 1619 Project, regardless of state standards, school board priorities, or any other considerations.

The usual cost barriers are eliminated: "And it's all free!" The project comes as a comprehensive package: curricula, guides, activities, a lesson plan, article summaries, a lexicon, and "opportunities to connect with New York Times journalists."

Exactly how many teachers have responded to the Pulitzer Center's invitation is known only to the Pulitzer Center, which as of this writing has declined to say. The closest we have to a number is a statement in the Pulitzer Center's 2019 Annual Report that notes, "Our partnership with The 1619 Project brought our curricular resources to some 3,500 classrooms."[3] A "Pulitzer Center Update" in December adds the detail that "teachers across all 50 states have accessed the Pulitzer Center educational resources since the project's launch, and many have shared their students' work by posting to Twitter and emailing student work to education@pulitzercenter.org." The update also says:

> *Educators from hundreds of schools and administrators from six school districts have also reached out to the Center for class sets of the magazine. Teachers are using the magazine in their classes to teach subjects ranging from English to History and Social Studies, and their engagement with the project has guided students in creating essays, poetry, visual art, performances, and live events that demonstrate their learning.*[4]

The 2019 Annual Report not only mentions 3,500 classrooms but also "tens of thousands of students in all 50 states engaged with the curricular resources."

Chapter Twelve

The Annual Report lists five (not six) "school systems that have adopted the Project "district-wide." These school districts, and enrollments in each, are as follows:

Buffalo, NY: 31,050 students in 2018–19

Chicago, IL: 355,156 students for the 2019–20 school year, as of November 8, 2019

Washington, DC: 49,103 students in 2018–19

Wilmington, DE: 40,794 students (est. based on three districts)

Winston-Salem, NC: 96,756 students in the 2013–14 school year[5]

Total: 572,859

So in those five districts alone we can assume that more than half a million school students have some exposure to the themes and materials of the 1619 Project, though doubtless the intensity of the exposure varies by grade level and by the commitment of the teachers.

In the fall of 2019, American public schools enrolled about 50.8 million students.[6] Thus, by its adoption in five large school districts, the 1619 Project reached only a little more than 1 percent of public-school students. It seems unlikely that the hit-and-miss approach of the Pulitzer Center reached more than a few tens of thousands elsewhere in the United States during the 2019–2020 school year (preceding school closures during the coronavirus pandemic). But a 1 percent penetration during the project's first year is significant. And September

2020 (whether schools are open or operating via online learning) may bring a different story. The *Times* and the Pulitzer Center have been building their base, and they are nothing if not committed. We can anticipate these numbers to grow.

A NEWSPAPER AS ARBITER OF HISTORY AND EDUCATION

The *Times* considers the 1619 Project to be, above all, an educational endeavor. It aims to teach America truths about the past that have been suppressed or that have, until now, never been told properly. The Pulitzer Center aims to implement that vision by convincing teachers and school districts to adopt 1619 curricula drawn from or based on the 1619 Project. The *Times*, in other words, indicts American schools, past and present, for teaching history poorly. Some of this alleged inadequacy stems from the alleged deliberate racism of white supremacist books and teachers, and some of it from ignorance of the story that the *Times* judges to be the real history of America.

This is a very unusual role for a newspaper. Journalists are generally not historians, and the *Times* made very limited and profoundly inadequate attempts to consult with relevant historians both before and after it published the 1619 Project. In ordinary news reporting, the identities of sources are a crucial element, and in writing history, historians are duty-bound to identify the documents they examined and the experts they relied on. The *Times* dispensed with these procedures in the 1619 Project, which only here and there names a source or explains the basis of an assertion. The 1619 Project is thus not legitimate journalism, and it isn't legitimate history either. It is mainly an assemblage of poorly sourced assertions – an extended opinion piece.

That does not necessarily mean all the assertions are false. The claim that schools have done a poor job of incorporating slavery and the history of African Americans into the broader topic of American history was true for the period from the Civil War through the mid-1960s. The quality of the instruction since then is a more complicated picture. A good way to evaluate the *Times'* claims about how American history has been taught over the generations is to consider the textbooks that have been used. The bulk of this chapter is a tour of those textbooks, concluding with a look at the new 1619 curriculum.

THE FRAUGHT HISTORY OF HISTORY TEXTBOOKS

According to the Pulitzer Center, "The 1619 Project tackles the subject of enslavement in a way that will be new to many American students." That seems likely. Few schools until now have been teaching that America was a "slavocracy"; that slavery is our founding institution; and that every salient characteristic of America today is the result of slavery.

But we must go back several generations to find school textbooks that truly soft-pedal the subject of the history of slavery. Cynthia Greenlee, who received her PhD in history from Duke University and specializes in "African-American women's and legal history of the late nineteenth and early twentieth centuries," usefully provides a tour of how schoolbooks at the turn of the last century dealt with slavery. Writing in *Vox*, she notes that "*Hazen's Elementary History of the United States: A Story and a Lesson*, a popular early 20th-century textbook for young readers" told "the story of the first black Virginians" upon their arrival in 1619: "'The settlers bought them,' explained the 1903 text, '... and found them so helpful in raising tobacco that more were brought in, and slavery became part of our history.'" Greenlee also notes the "distorted history" to be found in that era in "many Southern-focused textbooks [that] promoted a Lost Cause approach to Jamestown and slavery writ large." She cites, for example, "*A Child's History of North Carolina*, circa 1916, which also focused on slavery's profitability and erased its violence. In this view, the enslaved people were happy, and Southern slave owners were reluctant masters at best."[7]

Northern writers attempted "a more nuanced approach," but Greenlee finds these wanting as well. She gives as an example, from 1886, Henrietta Christian Wright's *Children's Stories of American Progress*, which imagines the perspective of the slaves arriving at Jamestown in 1619. They "looked wearily out from the port-holes of the ship" and saw a new landscape that "only seemed dreary and desolate, a land of exile and death." But Wright, says Greenlee, while "moralizing on slavery as an evil," still portrayed black people as inferior to whites. Greenlee also cites the endeavor by black educators to write their own history textbooks, beginning in 1890 when Edward A. Johnson published *A School History of the Negro Race in America from 1619–1819*. In these books slavery is treated frankly but as part of a "black past that was more than slavery."[8] Greenlee does not say nor do I have any way of determining exactly where and for how long these books were used. That information is generally absent from all such studies.

Greenlee skips over the middle decades of the twentieth century, but I can supply a relevant example from my own library. *Exploring American History*, by Connecticut schoolteacher Mabel B. Casner and Yale historian Ralph Henry Gabriel, was a textbook aimed at the upper grades. First published in 1931, it went through many editions into the 1950s. Casner and Gabriel exhibit their hostility and condescension toward African Americans every time the subject comes up, which is not that often in a nearly 800-page book. Here, they explain why overseers had to whip slaves:

> *It made no difference to slaves whether they did much or little during a day. They sometimes had to be driven to their tasks with a lash. The slaves, moreover, were ignorant and careless. The wise planter gave them only simple and strong tools to use, for they would break others.*

Here is how they explain the declining fortunes of cotton farms in South Carolina as the result of the agricultural practices of the slaves: "The soil of South Carolina, cultivated for years by ignorant and careless slaves, was beginning to wear out and was not bringing forth such large crops as it once had."[9]

Casner and Gabriel continue in this vein, noting that house slaves were "bound to each other by deep ties of affection" but that field slaves had "occasionally" to feel the whip on their backs. The slave trade "was one of the worst aspects of slavery," but after 1808 slaves were brought "mostly by New England sea-captains."[10] For the sake of accuracy, note that when the 1808 federal prohibition on the Atlantic slave trade went into effect, America had about 1.1 million slaves. That number grew to 3.9 million by 1860, but mostly through births. Of the 2.8 million increase, only 50,000 (1.7 percent) were contraband slaves brought to the United States in violation of the law.

The most demeaning parts of the textbook, however,

deal with Reconstruction, where Casner and Gabriel address the issue of "training those who had been slaves all their lives to use their freedom wisely." Many, they say, "found that freedom could be a greater curse than slavery." When blacks came to power in Southern states, disaster ensued: "The Negroes were ignorant, and most of the carpetbaggers were rascals." One can practically hear Casner and Gabriel breathe a sigh of relief when they describe the rise of the Ku Klux Klan and "the laws by which the Negro was kept from voting."[11]

Textbooks like this have not gone unnoticed. Donald Yacovone, who with Henry Louis Gates Jr. coauthored *The African Americans: Many Rivers to Cross* (2013), provides a tour of books of later vintage than those covered by Cynthia Greenlee. In his essay, "Teaching White Supremacy: U.S. History Textbooks and the Influence of Historians," Yacovone characterizes this genre of books as "white man's history."[12] Surely the label applies to Casner and Gabriel's *Exploring American History*, and Yacovone gets around to excoriating it, along with other Klan-apologist textbooks such as Marcus Jernegan's *The Growth of the American People* (1934):

> *According to Jernegan, the Klan did little more than play on the "superstitious fears of the negroes" and scared them at night by dressing in white sheets and shouting "Beware! The Great Cyclops is angry!" and thus discouraged blacks from voting. Accusations of real Klan violence, he asserted, were largely fabricated by Carpetbaggers and Scalawags.*

Indignation is a proper response to these sorts of books. But that indignation should be tempered by the realization that such books are long gone from the American classroom. The youngest living Americans who studied these books as schoolchildren are now in their late seventies.

In the 1950s American history textbooks moved beyond defending the Ku Klux Klan, but they still dealt timidly with race. A partial exception was *The Challenge of Democracy*, a McGraw-Hill textbook published circa 1951. As Joseph Moreau notes in *Schoolbook Nation: Conflicts over American History Textbooks from the Civil War to the Present*, the textbook's chapter on the Fair Employment Practices Commission (FEPC) describes it as "a federal agency set up in 1941 to guarantee equal rights for Blacks working in factories with war contracts." On learning that his state had adopted the book, the governor of Alabama intervened, and McGraw-Hill capitulated to the changes he wanted. Thereafter, "the FEPC virtually disappeared from history textbooks," writes Moreau, whose book recounts many such incidents.[13]

The incident also testifies to the quality of Moreau's research. With the original textbook nowhere to be found, Moreau, a history teacher at the Abraham Joshua Heschel School in New York City, bases his account on the "Minutes of the State Board of Education of Alabama, 22 May, 1952," in the state archives. Moreau, however, isn't the only researcher to have paid close attention to how textbooks presented African Americans in the 1950s and after. Dozens or perhaps hundreds have addressed the topic, having pored over thousands of American history textbooks published in the period.

THE ELUSIVENESS OF A COMMON NARRATIVE

I won't try to pioneer my own path through this wilderness but instead will rely on Moreau and a few others to capture the larger picture. Moreau's encompassing theme is that history textbooks have always been at the center of social and political disputes in the United States. There was never a time, he says, in which we had consensus on which story to tell or how to tell it. His foil for this thesis is Frances FitzGerald, a once widely read journalist and historian, who argued in *America Revised: History Schoolbooks in the Twentieth Century* (1979) that history textbooks had fallen off a multicultural cliff in the 1960s. FitzGerald says that the textbooks in use prior to the 1960s, whatever their differences, converged on a common-core narrative of the American past. But the textbooks of the 1960s, she says, are typically fragmented with stories meant to appeal to the pride of disparate ethnic groups.

FitzGerald was in the main right, or in Moreau's view, "half right."[14] She was right that there had been, for better or worse, an underlying unity among the older textbooks no matter how diverse their specific contents, and that the 1960s brought an end of that. But Moreau is right, too, in his observations that our history textbooks have always been a battlefield in which competing regional, political, religious, and ethnic groups have sought to promote their own views. What was new in the 1960s wasn't the arrival of conflict and disagreement; rather it was the loss of confidence on the part of textbook writers that the disagreements could be contained in a coherent story.

To refute FitzGerald, Moreau presents evidence of past conflicts that stood in the way of any common narrative. Crispus Attucks, the part-black sailor killed in the Boston Massacre, for example, became a favorite of textbook writers in the 1960s and after, but Moreau observes that Attucks first appeared in a textbook in the 1870s, in "a widely read text of the era, the *Young Folks' History of*

Chapter Twelve

the United States by Thomas Wentworth Higginson, former abolitionist, confidante of John Brown, and commander of the first regiment of African-American soldiers in the Civil War." Higginson's textbook inadvertently "inspired White Southerners, among them the former vice president of the Confederacy, to write their own histories of the South."[15] (Some of the books described by Cynthia Greenlee fit this category.) Thus, at least since the Civil War, sectionalism has played a large role in determining what American history textbooks say about African Americans.

One of Moreau's themes is that textbook publishers, ever alert to the danger of losing a market in the South, played down the nastiness of slavery, emphasized the problems in Reconstruction, and ignored all but the most banal aspects of African-American history since. Moreau's example of this minimizing approach is a 1953 textbook, *The United States: From Wilderness to World Power*, by Ralph Volney Harlow, which explains that plantation slaves enjoyed the advantage over factory workers because theirs was "healthful" outdoor work, with "a restful, two-hour break at midday." Moreau also cites I. James Quillen and Edward Krug's *Living in Our America* as an early 1950s textbook that minimizes slavery. Quillen and Krug mention "overseers who whipped the lazy and severely punished those who disobeyed the rules," but mostly they treat plantation life as congenial for all involved.[16]

Casner and Gabriel's KKK-defending 1931 textbook, *Exploring American* History, was reissued many times. It returned in 1950 with a more circumspect text, *Story of American Democracy*, which, as Moreau notes, devoted just a handful of sentences to the life of slaves. Shorn of their more egregious opinions, the authors offer such anodyne characterizations as, "The planter fed, clothed, and cared for his slaves. He took care of the old people when they could no longer work. Slavery made life in the South very different from life in the North."[17]

Moreau also corrals several textbooks from the 1950s that propagated the theme that Reconstruction was a disaster. Leon H. Canfield and Howard B. Wilder's 1959 textbook *The Making of Modern America* describes Reconstruction as a period of "shameful dishonesty and misrule" – as if they had gathered their material from D. W. Griffith's 1915 pro-Klan movie *The Birth of a Nation*. Canfield and Wilder's book is one of several examples cited by Moreau on the way to his broader observation that, post-Reconstruction, "African-Americans largely departed from textbooks, appearing infrequently or in awkward contexts."[18]

One of these books, however, plays a pivotal role in what came next.

THE NEW TEXTS OF THE 1960S

When Detroit Public Schools selected *Our United States: A Bulwark of Freedom* (1959), by Harold Ebling, Fred M. King, and James Harlow, as a history textbook, it provided the grounds for action that some black activists had been waiting for. It was a book that plainly demonstrated black exclusion: blacks appeared in illustrations three times, always as slaves, and, writes Moreau, "their contributions to the nation were mostly limited to music." A citizens' organization called Group on Advanced Leadership (GOAL) had already been organized to force the schools to adopt better textbooks. In 1962, Richard Henry, the head of GOAL, saw his son's copy of *Our United States* and decided it had the right combination of ignoring and caricaturing blacks to serve as exhibit A in a public campaign. GOAL, soon joined by the local branch of the NAACP, struck a chord. The NAACP described *Our United States* as presenting an "image of the Negro" as "a dependent, servile creature" who is "incapable of functioning as a responsible person."[19] Much the same could have been said of many other history textbooks of the time, but *Our United States* quickly became the exemplar of racist American history textbooks.

Meanwhile signs of progress had begun to appear. A 1961 textbook, *This Is Our Nation*, by Paul F. Booler and E. Jean Tilford, included a discussion of *Brown v. Board of Education* and the 1957 Civil Rights Act. Moreau cites this as moving beyond the era in which George Washington Carver and Booker T. Washington exhausted the list of post–Civil War blacks that attracted the attention of textbook writers. Generally, prior to 1962, he says, textbooks offered only "piecemeal and stilted attempts at inclusion."[20]

The Detroit activists, however, had found their moment. A year before, the Anti-Defamation League had issued a report by Lloyd Marcus, *The Treatment of Minorities in Secondary School Textbooks* (1961), that called attention to racial bias and stereotypes. Soon the Detroit protests were national news. Detroit's Board of Education, in the absence of any better textbooks, commissioned a short text of their own, *Struggle for Freedom and Right: The Negro in American History*. Publishers, says Moreau, "knew which way the wind was blowing." The larger northern cities were forming "an ideological bloc" to rival white conservatives in the South.[21]

Publishing a single textbook that could satisfy both sides appeared an impossibility. Publishers instead rushed in with textbooks that straddled the issues and satisfied nobody. Some quietly published two editions of each text, one for northern school districts and one for southern, allowing customers to believe that they were getting copies of a single, nationally accepted text. Black history appeared – at least in the northern editions – but it was not integrated into the main narratives of these books. It was splashed in as sidebars and anecdotes. The changes were nonetheless significant. Moreau notes the 1964 release of a new edition of Houghton Mifflin's *This Is America's Story*, advertised as featuring "civil rights demonstrations."[22]

Black writers of the period took note of the market opportunity. One of these was Lerone Bennett Jr., whose writings on black history had such a powerful influence on Hannah-Jones. But the signal event in this direction was the publication in 1966 of *Land of the Free*, by John W. Coughey, John Hope Franklin, and Ernest R. May. The book was a straightforward attempt to integrate blacks into mainstream American history, and it was tentatively adopted by the state of California. *Land of the Free* was a breakthrough, but it encountered strong pushback, primarily in a campaign against it launched by a California public education official. Reviewers (citizens who responded to an invitation to read the textbook and submit comments) were not always enthusiastic. Moreau quotes one who says, "The entire feeling of this book is that of the complete injustice of the white race toward the negro." *Land of the Free* featured figures that had not yet become standard parts of the American narrative but who soon would be, including Martin Luther King Jr. and Rosa Parks. "One couple objected to a whip-wielding overseer looming over a group of slaves. That scene, agreed another critic, 'is not typical, is very exaggerated and gives a wrong impression. Delete it as bias.'"[23]

The controversy surrounding *Land of the Free* didn't

stay in California, and it convinced publishers that they had to make more strenuous efforts to integrate blacks into American history textbooks. These efforts weren't always convincing. Moreau cites as an example Houghton Mifflin's 1978 textbook *These United States*, which features a sidebar about "Deborah Sampson, a woman of color who disguised herself as a man to fight in the Revolutionary War." Moreau describes this as a "strained effort" that upsets the "integrity of the story."[24]

Moreau cites a dozen or so other textbooks of the 1970s and 1980s in which the authors try their best to tell a story that encompasses black history as part of American history, but it appears a certain fragmentation remains. The one book he singles out for praise is Addison-Wesley's *U.S.A.: The American Experience* (1975), by Robert F. Madgic et al.: it "offered clear accounts of racist violence, which made its discussion of the Black Power movement in the 1960s refreshingly intelligible, in contrast to other, tamer books."[25]

In truth, in the major political, social, and economic developments of America before Emancipation, blacks were subordinate players: present but only as exceptions in positions to make consequential decisions. To cope with this truth, historians can shift the focus to everyday life; they can emphasize the importance of labor in the creation of wealth; and they can elevate the accomplishments of the relatively small number of free blacks. Or they can try, like the authors of the 1619 Project, to tear up the story and write a new one, one that rejects the idea that oppression and exploitation of blacks are parts of the American story and instead foregrounds them as central to the very meaning of America.

I have leaned heavily on Moreau for this period, but, as I said, he is only one of many writers who have attempted to synthesize what happened to American history textbooks in the post–World War II era. Alvin Wolf, an education professor at California State University, San Bernardino, for example, offers a harder-edged synthesis in "Minorities in U.S. History Textbooks, 1945–1985." Wolf sees racism in a textbook that asserts, "To live in the South was to live in daily fear of slave violence." The black perspective, says Wolf, would be, "To live in the South was to live in the daily hope of a successful rebellion against slave owners."[26] Robert Lerner, Althea K. Nagai, and Stanley Rothman published a study in 1995, *Molding the Good Citizen: The Politics of High School History Texts*, that offers a rigorous demonstration of Frances FitzGerald's thesis that something fundamental changed in the 1960s. What changed, according to Lerner, Nagai, and Rothman, was the willingness of schools to subordinate history instruction to the goal of promoting progressive social change. The textbook publishers merely fell in line. In his 2006 book *History in the Making: An Absorbing Look at How American History Has Changed in the Telling over the Last 200 Years*, Kyle Ward provides a vivid account of how textbooks differed dramatically in presenting the same material.[27] A more recent attempt to survey this landscape is Robin Lindley's "Textbooks and History Standards: An Historical Overview" (2013). Lindley confirms the views of Moreau, FitzGerald, and Wolf that the 1960s saw the dawn of a movement to publish history textbooks that replaced the antiblack bias of the past with a new attentiveness to overcoming stereotypes. She points to the influence of reports from the NAACP and other groups that "provided advice on detecting bias." But "as reformers urged school officials to offer textbooks that enhanced ethnic and racial pride," conservatives "called for a return to texts that celebrated American ideals, a Christian heritage and nationalism."[28]

This I take to be true but incomplete. Today it would be hard to find a mainstream American history textbook that fails to pay assiduous attention to blacks and other minorities. Frances FitzGerald lost her battle against multicultural fragmentation and her hope to restore a strong narrative focus to American history. Since then that battle has been fought repeatedly. It was in the forefront in 1994 when Lynne Cheney, who served as the chair of the National Endowment for the Humanities from 1986 to 1993, objected to the then newly drafted National Standards for United States History, slated for approval by the federal education bureaucracy. While she prevailed against standards that would have officially endorsed a multiculturalist interpretation of American history, teachers and textbook publishers generally fell in line behind the vision articulated in those standards by the historian and academic Gary Nash and his coauthors.[29] A similar battle erupted when the College Board revised its Advanced Placement US History Standards in 2014. Prominent historians objected, but the College Board went ahead with minimal changes.[30] Neither of these controversies was specifically about the place of black history in the American story, but both dealt with the transformation of American history that came as the result of efforts to incorporate minorities into a coherent narrative of the American past.

In this brief list of the highlights of the scholarship on American history textbooks, Frances FitzGerald's 1979 book *America Revised* deserves a little more attention. The book comprised three long essays originally published in *The New Yorker*. They were based on research she did in the collections of Columbia University's Teachers College, as well as extensive interviews with textbook writers and publishers. The book also includes an excellent bibliography of American history textbooks organized by decade of publication. In contending that group conflict has always been endemic to these textbooks, Moreau uses FitzGerald's work as a straw man, in effect discounting her beautifully detailed and intellectually subtle account of textbook history. FitzGerald by no means erases the past conflicts or argues, *pace* Moreau, that textbooks before the 1960s stuck to one simple story.

She writes, for instance, of how in the 1830s, "North American Indians are presented as interesting, important people," but they begin to diminish in prominence as the United States pushed actual Indians westward, until, "by the nineteen-thirties, the American memory, incarnate in history texts, had blocked out both the Indians and their fate." But then in the 1960s "many discoveries about Americans" appear, or in some cases, reappear: "The country [Americans] had conceived as male and Anglo-Saxon turned out to be filled with blacks, 'ethnics,' Indians, Asians, and women. . . . The country also turned out to be filled with Spanish-speaking people who had come from Mexico, Puerto Rico, and other countries of the Caribbean basin."[31] FitzGerald traces these abrupt changes not only to the "sudden upsurge of protest and equally sudden change of perspective among educators,"[32] but also to the growing influence of social science in history teaching and to a generation of teachers increasingly dominated by progressive ideology.

If you received an American education during the

1960s or the decades following, you can judge from your own recollections the degree to which textbooks and teachers provided a racially biased account of American history. My high school American history textbook was Thomas Bailey and David Kennedy's *The American Pageant*. How well it covered African-American history I cannot now say, but I recollect learning quite a bit about the horror of slavery, and what I learned in class was reinforced by popular culture.

For many, a high point of this pop-culture kind of extracurricular education was the acclaimed TV miniseries *Roots*, based on Alex Haley's 1976 novel *Roots: The Saga of an American Family*. Haley's book tells of the many generations of black Americans descended from Kunta Kinte, an eighteenth-century African, enslaved in Africa and sold to Americans. The eight-part miniseries aired on ABC during prime time on consecutive nights in January 1977 and had an estimated audience of more than 130 million viewers – 59 percent of the US population at the time. The last episode is judged to be the third-most-watched telecast in American history.[33] *Roots* vividly presents a version of the African-American past that reached far more people than any textbook ever did. It is, however, a work of fiction dressed up as fact. It excited welcome interest in a neglected topic but should not be mistaken as a reliable portrait of American slavery.

REACTION LEADS TO OVERREACTION

Looking back over the history of American history textbooks, we see plainly that several generations ago many of them combined neglect with bigotry in their treatment of slavery, racism, and African-American life. By the 1950s, very cautious and tepid efforts had begun to deal with these parts of the American past. Some publishers were more aggressive than others, but all were intimidated by the problem of marketing their books to schools in the South where they were met with a wall of hostility to anything that elevated attention to the evils of slavery or the existence of Jim Crow. By the early 1960s, civil rights activists both within and outside the black community were demanding changes in the textbooks and gaining political clout. A major correction was due, and textbook publishers attempted to comply with the demands. But the need was also addressed by writers such as Lerone Bennett, who published independent works that presented views of the African-American past that had little scholarly warrant. This vein of fanciful pseudo-history complicates the picture to this day, and it is part of the 1619 Project.

The effort by mainstream publishers to integrate black history into their textbooks stumbled in various ways. Relatively minor figures and events were shoehorned into larger narratives. Sidebars introduced human-interest stories of dubious connection to significant historical developments. Major lines of political, economic, scientific, diplomatic, military, intellectual, religious, and cultural history were dispensed with or radically diminished in favor of a new emphasis on social history. This entropy in the telling of American history came about as publishers struggled to determine how to revise the old story of America's triumphant rise over adversity to become the world's leading political and economic success. A new narrative of America as an oppressive state that exploited minorities and privileged a class of white supremacists could not be merged seamlessly with the old narrative. Incoherence was the inevitable result of trying to tell both stories at once.

Chapter Twelve

Surely there are ways to incorporate a forthright treatment of slavery, racism, and the black experience into the story of America's rise as a free, self-governing, creative, and prosperous nation. The key to doing that is to put the pursuit of the ideals of liberty and justice at the center of the story, with ample acknowledgment of how hard the struggle has been and how imperfect the results.

The 1619 Project should be seen in light of the reaction to the terribly inadequate history textbooks of seventy and more years ago. A major correction was needed, and it began in a serious way in 1966 with the publication of John Hope Franklin's *Land of the Free*. The 1619 Project carries the reaction into the realm of radical overreaction. It tells us, in effect, that we live in the land of the unfree, and it replaces the effort to tell a truthful history of America, with its failures as well as its achievements, with a story of nothing but failure.

TODAY'S TEXTS

But where are we today? Opinions differ. In 2018 Melinda Anderson, a freelance journalist who focuses on "critical issues of race, ethnicity, and equity in education," published an article in *The Atlantic*, "What Kids Are Really Learning about Slavery." It is essentially a reflection on the Southern Poverty Law Center's January 2018 report "Teaching Hard History: American Slavery," which I discussed in chapter 6. The report presents the results of a study that surveyed a thousand high school seniors and seventeen hundred social studies teachers and examined ten commonly used US history textbooks and fifteen sets of state standards. The study led to some heart-sinking findings, Anderson notes, such as that "only 8 percent" of high school seniors "could identify slavery as the cause of the Civil War."[34]

Wait a minute. If these students had studied the 1619 Project they would have learned that slavery was *not* the cause of the Civil War. Hannah-Jones is emphatic about that, and so too is Alex Lichtenstein, editor of *The American Historical Review*, in defending Hannah-Jones's thesis. It is small wonder, with the experts arguing with one another, that the students do not know the right answer.

The SPLC also discovered, Anderson further notes, that "fewer than one-quarter (22 percent) of participating high-school seniors knew that 'protections for slavery were embedded in [America's] founding documents' – that rather than a 'peculiar institution' of the South, slavery was a Constitutionally enshrined right."[35] This assertion takes us onto highly contentious ground. It has been the subject of nearly two centuries of debate whether the Constitution embeds slavery. Sean Wilentz argues in *No Property in Man* that the Constitution was written artfully to avoid mentioning slavery. One way to explain that reticence is that delegates from the northern states and some of their southern allies disliked slavery, but, to form a viable union, they had to work around the determination of Georgia and South Carolina to preserve the slave system.

Initially the Framers tried to assign to Congress the task of what to do about the Atlantic slave trade, but the delegates from Georgia and South Carolina anticipated that Congress would, in Jefferson's words, "immediately suppress the importation of slaves." Jefferson continued: "These two States, therefore, struck up a bargain with the three New England States. If they would join to admit slaves for some years, the southernmost States would join in changing the clause which required two-thirds of the legislature in any vote."[36]

Of the fifty-five delegates to the Constitutional Convention, more than thirty were slaveholders. They could easily have written slavery into the Constitution, but they veered away from doing so. That was partly due to northern opposition, but partly also due to the views of many of the slaveholders themselves – individuals who could be called antislavery slaveholders because they saw slavery as a necessary evil or temporary expedient, something that would gradually wither away. It was an issue whose resolution could be put off, with most accepting the view that the future of slavery would be decided by the states. The battle, however, was over slavery's extension and whether Congress had a right to prohibit slavery in the territories.

Slavery was thus "embedded" in the nation's founding documents not in the spirit of general approbation but fraught with suppressed conflict. To say, as Anderson does in endorsing the SPLC report's assumptions, that slavery was "a Constitutionally enshrined right" is misleading at best. Slavery was actively discussed in the constitutional debates, and it is addressed via circumlocutions in the Constitution itself; but as Wilentz puts it in *No Property in Man*, "by affirming that it would be wrong, as James Madison did at the Constitutional Convention, 'to admit in the Constitution the idea that there could be property in men,' the founders left room for political efforts aimed at slavery's restriction and, eventually, its destruction, even under a Constitution that safeguarded slavery."[37]

Of course, some eagerly misinterpret the "three-fifths clause" – meant to limit the congressional power of the slave states – as a tacit endorsement of slavery. The clause itself referred to "three-fifths of other persons" – meaning slaves – to count toward the apportionment of seats in the House of Representatives. Without that provision, the slave states would have gained an overwhelming majority of seats in the House while, of course, denying the vote to their slaves. The avoidance of the word "slaves" was deliberate. The Founders did not want to write the institution of slavery into the Constitution, but they needed to reckon with the reality of the day.

So the 22 percent of high school seniors who said that slavery is embedded in the Constitution were technically correct, although the other 78 percent don't illustrate a "failure to grasp key concepts underpinning the nature and legacy of slavery," as Anderson maintains. In fact to say that slavery is not embedded in the Constitution is in keeping with the Founders' intent as well. Anderson's article is instructive in that it does provide some cringe-worthy examples of awful classroom practices, including that "a class of middle-schoolers in Charlotte, North Carolina, was asked to cite 'four reasons why Africans made good slaves.'"[38]

What are or what were American students learning about slavery prior to the 1619 Project? We know from Hannah-Jones's reflections that back in high school her teacher introduced her to the writings of Lerone Bennett Jr., some of whose egregious misrepresentations of American history became her bedrock beliefs. We know that Howard Zinn's *People's History of the United States* has become one of the most popular textbooks in the country. Chapter 9 of Zinn's book, "Slavery Without Submission, Emancipation Without Freedom," spares no detail about the brutality and the inhumanity of the institution. But Zinn also emphasizes the determination of the slaves to hold onto their families and their personal dignity: "Slaves hung on determinedly to their selves, to their love of family, their wholeness. A shoemaker on the South Carolina Sea Islands expressed this in his own way: 'I'se lost an arm but it hasn't gone out of my brains.'"[39] While Zinn's textbook has many flaws, neglecting slavery is not one of them, and millions of American students have encountered the history of slavery through Zinn if not elsewhere in their studies.

Mainstream history textbooks, however, also now provide full, detailed accounts of slavery. One of the most popular American history textbooks used in high school today is *America's History*, by James A. Henretta, Eric Hinderaker, Rebecca Edwards, and Robert O. Self.[40] The index lists eighty-four entries under "slaves," "slavery," and "slave trade," and all told slavery appears on more than a hundred pages of this thousand-page textbook. It is also richly illustrated. *America's History*, in my view, is a textbook with a somewhat sour view of America, but it cannot be faulted for its treatment of slavery, emancipation, or American blacks during and after that period.

I say it cannot be faulted, but of course the 1619 Project does fault it, because *America's History* does not endorse the idea that America's history needs to be reframed by putting slavery at the center of everything, and it does not endorse the view that America was a "slavocracy."

LESSON PLANS

There is no substitute for going to the Pulitzer Center's website and reading through the material that is provided for classroom instruction, and in any case the effort to summarize it would capsize this book. One example of what it offers is a "Lesson Plan: Exploring 'The Idea of America' by Nikole Hannah-Jones." This lesson plan is dated August 13, 2019, five days before the publication of the 1619 Project, and it is labeled "All Grades." There is presumably something here that can be taught to primary school students as well as high school seniors.

The lesson plan has several parts, among them the full text of Hannah-Jones's essay, "The Idea of America." The "Lesson Overview" is faithful to the essay. It explains:

> *The 1619 Project, inaugurated with a special issue of* The New York Times Magazine, *challenges us to reframe U.S. history by marking the year when the first enslaved Africans arrived on Virginia soil as its foundational date.*
>
> *Award-winning investigative journalist Nikole Hannah-Jones provides an expansive essay on why "black Americans, as much as those men cast in alabaster in the nation's capital, are this nation's true 'founding fathers.'" Her essay chronicles a history of policies enacted to profit from and disenfranchise black Americans, and the fight not only to claim black liberation, but also to make liberation possible for all Americans.*

Students are offered a "warm-up" consisting of a few questions, such as, "What are the values stated in the Declaration of Independence?" The students then move on to "Introductory Reading and Discussion," some of which is intriguing: "Why do you think Nikole Hannah-Jones and other contributors to this issue chose to publish this work in *The New York Times Magazine*, a national news publication? What is journalism's role in shaping national memory?"[41]

First, though the editors of the *Times* now think otherwise, journalists are supposed to report the news and, where necessary, summarize the relevant background in an unbiased way. They are not a proper vehicle for "reframing history." That's because history is more than telling a story. It requires a scrupulous attention to the facts, to the uncertainties, and to the genuine conflicts of interpretation among experts. The *Times*, a news organization that assigned journalists rather than historians to write history, failed on all of these criteria.

Second, teaching students the importance of the *Times* and the role of journalists "in shaping national memory" might not strike the average person as central to teaching American history, but we are not just *teaching* American history in the 1619 Project, we are "reframing" it.

Things get even more interesting in the next section, "In-depth Reading and Discussion." This includes tools such as a "graphic organizer tracking evidence Hannah-Jones provides for her central thesis." What follows are ten questions, commencing with these two:

> 1. *What examples of hypocrisy in the founding of the U.S. does Hannah-Jones supply? What evidence can you see for how "some might argue that this nation was founded not as a democracy but as a slavocracy"?*

> 2. *Why do you think Hannah-Jones consistently refers to what are commonly known as "plantations," such as Monticello, by the term "forced-labor camps" instead? Does any other language she uses to describe places, people, or events surprise or stand out to you?*[42]

The best way to end this chapter, I think, is to invite the reader to ponder the Pulitzer Center's questions and the possible answers. The 1619 Project aims to transform American education, if not all of American society. Teaching students to see "hypocrisy" in the Founding ought not to be too difficult. Teenagers are by nature inclined to see hypocrisy everywhere in the adult world.

Intensifying that predisposition and giving full scope to a cynical reading of the American past might well be the path to success for the curriculum based on the project.

Cynicism reveals some things, but it hides others, such as self-restraint, self-sacrifice, and commitment to the common good. The 1619 Project renders qualities like that invisible, and from what I have seen so far of the curriculum, it will only further the sorry idea that America is the low road, where wealth and power crush the innocent, and where racism is and always was the dominant ideology.

CHAPTER THIRTEEN

THE FUTURE

I F THE 1619 PROJECT were a term paper, any knowl-
edgeable, fair-minded teacher would give it an F and
be done with it. It demonstrates not only incompetence
in handling basic facts, but also a total disregard for the
importance of using reliable sources. The author of the
term paper displays wild overconfidence in her opinions
and rushes past points that she should have and easily
could have checked. Lack of intellectual modesty is not
necessarily a flaw in a term paper, but it is when it leads
the student to make brazen assertions that happen to be
false. Worse still is when the student chooses to draw on
long-discredited sources while ignoring the leading scholars in the field.

But the 1619 Project isn't an incompetent term paper.
It is a major declaration by the nation's "newspaper of
record," with a plan to make its claims the basis for the
teaching of US history in our schools. There is no single,
final authority to declare this project a failure – there are
only the many historians and others who have publicly
criticized the project for its errors and its subversive aims,
voicing those criticisms individually and together in
hopes of exposing the project's failings to the public.

There is no single, final authority who can say once

and for all whether George Washington chopped down that cherry tree. Historians tell us that it was a fable made up by Parson Weems in his 1800 biography of the late president. But there is nothing to stop some Americans from trusting that Weems's story is true, even if no primary source has ever corroborated it. Maybe the story is "true" in the sense that it faithfully captures the essential honesty of the six-year-old child who would become General and then President Washington.

When CBS News finally admitted that the six documents that Dan Rather had presented in September 2004 concerning President George W. Bush's service in the Texas Air National Guard in 1972–73 were not authentic, the *New York Times* headlined the story "Memos on Bush Are Fake but Accurate, Typist Says."[1] The story was open to several possible interpretations: the documents weren't real but they told a true story; the documents and the story were false, but they captured a deeper truth; or the documents were false and the story misleading, but they contained bits of the truth.

In any case, the error, which essentially ended Dan Rather's career, gave us the durable phrase "fake but accurate," which bears some connection to the more recently popular accusation "fake news," that is, deliberate misinformation. "Fake but accurate" is also kindred to Alexandria Ocasio-Cortez's explanation when caught in a false claim that the costs of her Medicare for All proposal could be covered by $21 trillion in "Pentagon accounting errors." The congresswoman said, "There's a lot of people more concerned about being precisely, factually, and semantically correct than about being morally right."[2]

Fake news is not necessarily unpopular news. A remark by Michael Radutzky, a producer for CBS's *60 Minutes*, has been widely quoted: "We're using the term 'fake news' to describe stories that are provably false, have enormous traction in the culture, and are consumed by millions of people."[3] By that definition, the 1619 Project is plainly fake news. Parts of it are "provably false," it has already gained enormous traction in the culture, and it has been widely read and discussed. Such a large project, of course, contains a great deal that is not false. A pirate ship really did bring slaves to Virginia in August 1619. Slavery really did become an entrenched American institution in some colonies that became states during the eighteenth century. Cotton plantations in the American South really were in many cases hugely profitable, and cotton really did become a major American export. And Abraham Lincoln really did meet in the White House with five black leaders (and a white reporter) to discuss the possibility of sending freed slaves abroad to create a colony. It's not that these things didn't happen. George W. Bush did, in fact, serve in the Texas Air National Guard as well. The "fake news" comes in when such facts are bent and twisted to tell a story that is provably false.

It is not true that the arrival of slaves on the *White Lion* was the beginning of chattel slavery in America, where it was widespread before Columbus, or in Virginia, where those slaves may have become indentured servants once debarking in the Chesapeake. It is not true that the American Revolution was fought to protect slavery. It is not true that cotton production was the foundation of American wealth in the nineteenth century, or that the plantations were the guiding model and origin of American capitalism. It is not true that Lincoln was a racist hell-bent on sending blacks back to an Africa they had never seen and that could not be considered their home.

Faced with the factual inaccuracy of key assertions in

the 1619 Project, many who championed it and others who welcomed it on less ardent but still friendly terms fell back on a version of "fake but accurate." They say, in effect, "All right, Hannah-Jones and some of the others messed up some details, but that doesn't undermine the larger importance of the project." Another line of defense that is often offered says, "The 1619 Project is only the beginning of a conversation. Sometimes you have to exaggerate a little to get the conversation going, but see? Now we are having that conversation, unlike before when no one talked about slavery or race."

The fake-but-accurate defense and the it's-a-needed-conversation defense of the 1619 Project are both climb-downs from the shrill assertiveness of Jake Silverstein's and Nikole Hannah-Jones's original positions. Nor do such defenses comport with the industry put in motion to distribute the project even before the *Times* published it. Those climb-downs may be enough to keep the partisans of the 1619 Project marching forward, and also enough to maintain the credibility of the project in the eyes of those who take it as more an expression of a sensibility than a set of specific claims about American history. The sensibility is, by now, a familiar one: "Never mind the exact details, we know America was a rough place, where European settlers mistreated the native population, ravaged the environment, enslaved blacks, and put in place institutionalized inequality and oppression that continues to this day."

AN EMPHASIS ON 1776

Insisting on mere accuracy is unlikely to sway people whose sensibility has been formed along these lines. How then is the 1619 Project to be defeated? One possible

Chapter Thirteen

answer is the work of Robert Woodson and the Woodson Center, based in Washington, DC. Woodson is a humanitarian, a community-development advocate, and a civil-rights activist known for his efforts to stem youth violence. He is the editor of two books, *Youth Crime and Urban Policy: A View from the Inner City* (1981) and *On the Road to Economic Freedom: An Agenda for Black Progress* (1987), and the author of *The Triumphs of Joseph: How Today's Community Healers Are Reviving Our Streets and Neighborhoods* (1998). He was also among the first national figures to criticize the *Times'* initiative.

Ten days after the magazine presented the 1619 Project, Woodson published an op-ed in the *Wall Street Journal* arguing that the project would hurt blacks by encouraging a sense of victimhood. He immediately discerned the core theme of the project: "Whites have always been and continue to be the beneficiaries of both slavery and its attendant institutional racism – and blacks the perpetual victims." He anticipated the positive media coverage and the eagerness of "left-leaning politicians" to associate themselves with it. And he recognized the importance of the educational angle: "Most dangerous of all, the Pulitzer Center has packaged the *Times'* project as a curriculum for students of all ages that will be disseminated throughout the country." He also called on leaders within the black community to voice criticisms of the 1619 Project, lest the idea sink in further that "blacks are born inherently damaged by an all-prevailing racism and that their future prospects are determined by the whims of whites."[4]

A few weeks after Woodson published this, I ran into him at an event, and he told me that he was planning to launch a project of his own through the Woodson Center. That project has come to be known simply as "1776," or "1776 Unites." I told him my organization was working on a response we called the "1620 Project." Arguably, Woodson hit on the better name for an endeavor to remind Americans that our nation was founded on the pursuit of freedom, not on slavery and racism. Most Americans connect easily with 1776 as the signal moment in our history; in focusing on 1620, we run into the problem that the Pilgrims in that pre-Enlightenment age did not talk about natural rights in our modern, secular sense. Some of the essential ingredients of America had yet to be cultivated. Woodson has the benefit of a project that truly goes to those essentials. He has also stayed true to the goal of rallying black leaders and intellectuals to resist the *Times*' 1619 onslaught.

In February 2020, Woodson's 1776, described on its website as "an assembly of independent voices who uphold our country's authentic founding virtues and values and challenge those who assert America is forever defined by its past failures, such as slavery," was formally launched.[5] Woodson published another powerful op-ed in which he wrote: "The purveyors of animosity have fine-tuned their strategy on this issue, creating a villain composed of 'white privilege' and 'institutional racism' that must be countered through a game plan of entitlements and reparations for its victims." He has successfully pulled together a group of "black scholars and social activists," but not to combat the 1619 Project directly: "Rather than giving point-by-point counterarguments to the findings and conclusion of the 1619 Project, our focus will be to identify and highlight solutions, models of success in reviving our streets and communities, and actionable goals that should be pursued."[6]

When I next spoke with him, Woodson reiterated his view that there is not much to gain by criticizing the 1619 Project with any specificity or in singling out Hannah-

Jones or others for their errors. In this Woodson's plan differs a great deal from my own. I see the merits of his "debunking the myth that slavery is the source of present-day disparities and injustice" by focusing on "people who have succeeded in the face of daunting obstacles." But I think there is also an important part to be played by those of us who bring to light the mendacity and manipulation that lie at the heart of the 1619 Project. Although I have chosen a very different approach from Woodson's, I believe each can complement the other.

A MATTER OF IDEOLOGY?

I am mindful, however, that not everyone agrees that the project's mistakes are either that important or that compromising to the project as a whole. Adam Serwer, a staff writer for *The Atlantic*, wrote a long essay about the historians who signed the letter to the *Times* protesting the project's errors and other historians who declined to sign the letter. Serwer depicts the disagreements as matters of ideology, not historical veracity. "Some historians," he writes, wondered whether the historians' letter aimed "to discredit laymen who challenged an interpretation of American national identity."[7] By "laymen" Serwer means the journalists and other nonhistorians who wrote most of the essays in the 1619 Project.

The choice Serwer sets up between ideology and veracity is unnecessary. We can challenge the factual basis of the 1619 Project and also, like Robert Woodson, criticize its interpretation of history. This book does both, as have many of the historians I have quoted along the way. Other historians who have declined to speak out, knowing full well that some of the essays in the 1619 Project are rife with major historical inaccuracies, have found excuses, not reasons, for remaining silent. Serwer interviewed a number of them.

Serwer does pinpoint the "ideological" divide, if we want to call it that:

> *The clash between the* Times *authors and their historian critics represents a fundamental disagreement over the trajectory of American society. Was America founded as a slavocracy, and are current racial inequities the natural outgrowth of that? Or was America conceived in liberty, a nation haltingly redeeming itself through its founding principles?*[8]

But to phrase the disagreement as "fundamental" is to concede the matter to hapless relativism. There is an answer to the question, "Was America founded as a slavocracy?" – an answer in actual, documented history that does not depend on surmises or interpretative leaps. And the answer is, No, it was not founded as a slavocracy. It wasn't founded as a slavocracy in Virginia in 1619, or at Plymouth in 1620, or in Philadelphia in 1776. We can perhaps conjure other dates from history that have some lesser claim to be "founding" events, but there is no plausible case for an American founding that makes "slavocracy" the beginning of the story or the main charter for what followed.

To the question, "Or was America conceived in liberty, a nation haltingly redeeming itself through its founding principles?" the answer is, Yes, though the story is definitely complicated, particularly by slavery. Slavery contradicted the love of liberty and equality, but globally, on all habitable continents, it had millennia of practice and theory behind it. It perversely fell within the rule of law until the laws were changed. To tell the story of America requires telling how those laws were changed, and how resistance to changing them was overcome.

Serwer, citing the Southern Poverty Law Center study discussed in chapter 12, observes that "few American high-school students know that slavery was the cause of the Civil War, that the Constitution protected slavery without explicitly mentioning it, or that ending slavery required a constitutional amendment."[9] As I noted in chapter 12, this ignorance doesn't stem from a suppression of the story of slavery in the teaching of history in our schools. The problem is that American schools do a terrible job of teaching American history in general. Except for the students who sign up for Advanced Placement US History, our schools simply let American history wash away in the tide of "social studies." And it is worth saying again that teaching the 1619 Project – which, in an irony that seems lost on Serwer and others, itself states that slavery wasn't the cause of the Civil War – is not likely to rectify this profound problem. If anything, it will worsen it by making history the pivot of victimology and group resentments.

Serwer hits one more chord worth noting. He says the great divide between 1619 Project supporters and detractors has to do with

> the argument that anti-black racism is a more intractable problem than most Americans are willing to admit. A major theme of the 1619 Project is that the progress that has been made has been fragile and reversible – and has been achieved in spite of the nation's true founding principles, which are not the lofty ideals few Americans genuinely believe in.

He has something here. He spoke to Nell Irvin Painter, a retired Princeton historian who objected to the project's portrayal of the 1619 Africans in Virginia as slaves but wouldn't sign the historians' letter. "I felt that if I signed on to that, I would be signing on to the white guy's attack of something that has given a lot of black journalists and writers a chance to speak up in a really big way," she told Serwer. "So I support the 1619 Project as kind of a cultural event."[10]

I have trouble finding any sympathy for Painter's view, which condescends to black journalists as needing an exemption from the standard of accuracy in order "to speak up in a really big way." The way to correct mythical versions of the past is to tell the truth; launching a counter-myth is foolishness. But I suspect that Painter's view is shared among many left-of-center historians, who package their criticisms of the details of the project with assurances that the project itself is a great idea.

It isn't. The 1619 Project as a whole is myth-making aimed at intensifying identity politics and group grievance. It doesn't aim, as it says, to tell "our story truthfully." It aims to tell it with falsehoods and deceptions for the purpose of instilling resentment.

WHAT SHOULD WE DO?

A reader who has accompanied me this far may hope for some proposed solutions to the problems posed by the introduction of the 1619 Project into our national debate. Some other readers, impatient for a bottom line, may have skipped all that precedes in search of my "real" agenda. The attentive reader has the advantage on this point because my real agenda is to illuminate what the 1619 Project means for America. I have not hidden my view that the *Times* has a large advantage over those of us who think the project will damage America, perhaps severely. The 1619 Project's advantages include long-term planning, abundant financial and other resources, and an army of activists many of whom are well placed as teachers or in other professions to advance the cause.

We doubters have come late to the game and have far less to work with. We are also far less cohesive. For example, *National Review Online* published a piece by a historian that conjures moral equivalency between the 1619 Project and those who criticize it. We critics, the author says, are just as simplistic as the 1619ers. He prefers a story of no fixed past, but only perpetual conflict:

> *Whether the subject is slavery or liberty, American history is a story of contested principles. A single birth year cannot unlock the very meaning of the nation, not least because how historians and others explain the past hinges on how they understand the present. An overemphasis on 1619, 1620, or any other year, makes our history far too simple.*

It is hard to imagine that someone who thinks like that will play any constructive role in resisting the corruption of our schools in the direction of the 1619 project's slavery-is-the-foundation-of-everything-in-this-vile-white-supremacist-society curriculum. As for 1620, he scoffs, "Like English colonists elsewhere, the Pilgrims and their descendants then stripped Native populations of their land through dubious property transactions and episodic wars." Plymouth's "settlers eked out a living on land of dubious fertility, and other colonies came to dwarf it in terms of population, economic clout, and military power. Ready to tell new stories about the American past, academic historians eventually kicked the Pilgrims to the scholarly curb."[11] Well, yes, a good many academic historians have done just that, which is a good reason to revisit the question. I don't contend that we can glimpse all of American history in the Mayflower Compact. But it serves as one of the useful starting points, and, as I've argued, a more productive starting point than the arrival of the *White Lion* with its human cargo in Virginia the year before.

In these pages I have cited dozens of prominent historians and other observers, and I've provided an account to date of the public-interest groups that have risen to the challenge of explaining why the 1619 Project poses a particular danger to America. But what should we do?

Ideally, we should rouse local school-board members who are in a position to say no to the 1619 curriculum. We should rally behind the Ashbrook Center's programs for teaching teachers American history and civics. And we should establish and promote similar efforts elsewhere. We should create curricula that offer strong alternatives to the 1619 Project. We should help philanthropic bodies find the right places to invest their resources. We should work at the state level in all fifty states to ensure that genuine American history and Western civilization general-education requirements are adopted and enforced. We should revisit requirements for teacher licensure to make sure they are not tilting in any ideological direction. We might urge states to revisit their curricular frameworks to be sure they are focused on substance, not attitude. We might endorse an external test for high school graduation.

All this is possible, but I don't want to lift the veil of pessimism just yet. None of these things will be done unless the American public first sees the need. You and I have to believe it is worth the fight.

Chapter Thirteen

WHAT'S AT STAKE

The 1619 Project isn't "fake but accurate." In crucial ways, it is fake and *in*accurate. This book is focused on two of the project's ten main essays in the original *New York Times Magazine* special issue. The remaining eight vary in quality. Several of them strain to find historical connections between current policies and slavery or the racial discrimination of the postslavery era. The topics of those eight essays are health insurance, traffic jams, the Tea Party, medical practice, black music, sugar in the American diet, incarceration, and the racial wealth gap. I commend the one on black music. The others sometimes present powerful stories about barbarous acts perpetrated on innocent men and women, but they typically make hairpin turns into broad generalizations and tendentious arguments that consistently align with leftist political goals. Reading through these articles gives the impression that white supremacy lies at the bottom of every inequity, real or imagined, in contemporary society. These essays have been subject to scattered rebuttals, but nothing like the multiple refutations prompted by the essays by Nikole Hannah-Jones and Matthew Desmond.

Those other essays deserve attention in their own right, but it is important not to lose sight of the larger picture. Silverstein, Hannah-Jones, and Desmond drag the entire project toward the conclusion that all the ills of America are the result of incurable white racism.

That is not a new "conversation" that has somehow been smothered or neglected for generations. It is a diatribe that has been recycled by black nationalists for half a century, and that has its own substantial literature. Hannah-Jones herself pays homage frequently to the writings of Lerone Bennett Jr., whose major works appeared in the 1960s and are still in print (he died in 2018). In an earlier chapter I drew attention to Bennett's marginal standing among mainstream historians, but it is fair to say that he was part of a movement among American historians to refocus American history on the faults and failures of the nation. This has been the dominant strain of academic history for almost half a century, but it failed to become the story that Americans outside the academy really believe. The 1619 Project aims to change that by conferring seemingly mainstream authority on a strand of radical disaffection with America. And it supplies the advocates of this narrative with the resources to amplify it in the media and the schools across the country.

Let's take several steps back. *History* is not just a collection of facts about the past, nor is it just "what happened." The study of history has standards and approved methods. It is a discipline. It is also the way in which our civilization thinks itself into existence. By means of history, we recognize how we came to be, what we are, and why that matters. The term that contrasts most strikingly with history is *mythology*, that is, stories of the past that express key values but that are not grounded in fact. Humanity the world over possesses mythology, but history is a cultural rarity. Our possession of history since the time of Herodotus and the Hebrews, the founders of secular and sacred history, has set us – Western civilization – apart from the ahistorical horizons of other peoples.

American history is important not just because we are Americans but because we Americans have so little to substantiate our common identity. The little we do have is a few hundred years of not-quite-shared experience as settlers and nation-builders. Within that history stand a mere handful of defining events that gave us the most dynamic society in human history. The principles that made that society possible and allow it to flourish today are embedded in our relatively short history. Not to know that history is not to grasp those principles.

The 1619 Project is, arguably, part of a larger effort to destroy America by people who find our nation unbearably bad. The project treats the founding principles of our nation as an illusion – a contemptible illusion. In their place is a single idea: that America was founded on racist exploitation. The form of this racist exploitation has shifted from time to time, from chattel slavery to free-market mechanisms, but its character has not changed at all. There is no American history as such, but only an eternal present consisting of white supremacy and black suffering. The 1619 Project thus consists of an effort to destroy America by teaching children that America never really existed, except as a lie told by white people in an effort to control black people. It eradicates American history and American values in one sweep.

The *New York Times*' decision to launch this project in 2019 and to continue it indefinitely probably reflects the confluence of several motives. Among these were (1) the appeasement of angry and aggressive members of the *Times*' staff who for the three years preceding the project's publication plagued *Times* management with complaints about the newspaper's failure to devote more time, space, and money to advance their vision of racial justice; (2) the social-justice agenda of the *Times* management itself, which feels that it has no legitimate basis for resisting the claims of the black activists; (3) the hope of energizing the Democratic electorate to oppose Trump in the 2020 election; (4) the failure of the Mueller investigation to deliver the results that the *Times* eagerly anticipated (the 1619 Project was intended as part of what *New York Times* executive editor Dean Baquet called a "pivot," from Trump as Russian collusionist to Trump as the face of white supremacy); (5) the desire to push government to pay reparations to blacks for slavery, as explicitly avowed by Nikole Hannah-Jones, the architect of the project; (6) postnationalism, that is, the idea that America is not exceptional and really shouldn't exist at all, to which end borders should be abolished and the oppressed should, finally, dispossess those who have "hoarded" their "white privilege" as "a thing of value";[12] and (7) the elevation of identity politics based on racial grievance to become the dominant or perhaps exclusive cultural construct bearing on the nation's politics, economics, and morality.

I have no way to say which of these were the strongest motives in setting the project in motion, though the disappointment with Mueller and the desire to pivot to racial issues in the 2020 election were plainly secondary, since the project began in January 2019, well before those motives emerged.

Making slavery the distinguishing aspect of American history creates an unbridgeable divide between blacks and whites. If the 1619 Project succeeds, it would revitalize racial antagonism – in both directions. It would also infantilize black Americans by teaching them that nothing they have ever done has changed their oppressed status one bit. The 1619 Project teaches that they have no friends or allies, and must rely only on themselves. The practical effects will in the short run be more affirmative action; in the longer run, reparations; and in the longest run, a version of racial separation promoted by black activists such as we now see at our universities.[13]

Americans should know their history. That's our best

defense against malicious myth-making. Reading history books is not to everyone's taste, which is a good reason why children should be taught history – so that they know some of it even if they don't pursue it as adults. A citizen should grow up knowing we are a free people under the rule of law. A citizen should know that it is not some happy accident but the result of an immense effort over many generations. It was the work of courageous men and women who pursued principle even when the situation seemed hopeless.

And Americans should certainly learn about slavery. All Americans should learn that the struggle to end slavery across the globe started in Western culture and was advanced by the United States. All Americans should learn that Vermont has pride of place in being the first government in the world to abolish slavery by constitutional dictum. All Americans should learn that ending slavery was a complex and severe struggle to realize our ideals of freedom and equality. As a people, we should take pride in abolition and the many steps taken beyond abolition to create a nation that extends equally to every citizen the blessings of liberty and justice.

POSTSCRIPT

In JANUARY 2020, when Roger Kimball, publisher of
Encounter Books, proposed the idea of my writing a
book about the 1619 Project, it was far from clear that
the controversy would continue long enough to warrant
a book-length response. But because I believed the larger
issues would linger even if the 1619 Project faded, I
agreed. I wrote the original version in March and early
April, and benefited from the uninterrupted time granted
by the national shutdown, which started in New York
City on March 16.

I mention these details because the book itself reflects
them. It describes the 1619 Project from the vantage point
of spring 2020, before other key developments. During
editing I was able to glance at some of these developments: Nikole Hannah-Jones won a Pulitzer Prize for the
1619 Project; and she proudly accepted the term "the
1619 Riots" as the name for the orgy of destruction that
followed the death of George Floyd in police custody. But
the river of 1619 news keeps rushing onward. As I write
now at the end of July, Hannah-Jones has again captured
wide attention with a series of tweets in which she asserts
that the 1619 Project was never intended to be "history."

This is an astonishing assertion eleven months after

her launching what she claimed at the time was an attempt to "reframe" American history and to tell the "truth" for the first time. Here is Hannah-Jones on July 27, 2020, flatly reversing herself: "I've always said that the 1619 Project is not a history. It is a work of journalism that explicitly seeks to challenge the national narrative and, therefore, the national memory. The project has always been as much about the present as it is the past." This wasn't a one-off statement. She reiterated it in a series of tweets, including this: "The crazy thing is, the 1619 Project is using history and reporting to make an argument. It never pretended to be a history. We explicitly state our aims and produced a series of essays. Critique was always expected, but the need to discredit it speaks to something else." And this: "Further, the curriculum is supplementary and cannot and was never intended to supplant US history curriculum (which is pretty terrible but none of these folks seem concerned about that.) Teachers have used it in English, social studies, art, foods classes." And this: "The fight here is about who gets to control the national narrative, and therefore, the nation's shared memory of itself. One group has monopolized this for too long in order to create this myth of exceptionalism. If their version is true, what do they have to fear of 1619?"[1]

It would be tedious to go back and count the dozens, perhaps hundreds, of times that Hannah-Jones herself, the *New York Times*, and the Pulitzer Center explicitly presented the 1619 Project as a work of history. Jonathan Butcher at the Heritage Foundation has begun to keep a list of instances in which Hannah-Jones plainly described her work as history. Here she is, for example, on National Public Radio's *Fresh Air*: "And on top of that was the pressure of having to try to get this right, that if we were

Postscript

going to undertake this project to try to tell this 400-year sweep of history of people who have been so intensely marginalized both in society and in popular media, that the pressure to do it justice was very high."[2]

What accounts for Hannah-Jones's sudden reversal after she and her colleagues had spent nearly a year fiercely defending the accuracy of her error-ridden essay? My guess is that she is doing a victory lap. At this point the popular success of the 1619 Project is so well established that she no longer needs to claim historical accuracy. She has moved on to something bigger: a narrative that is indeed reframing the whole idea of the American past. A false narrative that people believe is usually called a myth. Hannah-Jones is using several other terms: journalism, narrative, and above all "memory." Can we have a memory of things that never actually happened? Those are usually called "false memories," but they aren't typically awarded Pulitzer Prizes.

Surely by the time this book appears in print, the river of 1619 developments will have thrown up new surprises. I have to trust that the critique presented here will stand on its own merits even if it necessarily trails fresh outrages against scholarship and the facts. I will also no doubt miss important developments among the critics of the 1619 Project. The organizations I mentioned in chapter 6 as working on public critiques of the project have all moved forward in their work. And individual scholars and critics have published some brilliant critiques of the project. To mention but one, Rod Dreher, in "What Is The 1619 Omelet?," builds a devastating parallel between the false reporting of "Walter Duranty, the *New York Times*'s Pulitzer-winning Moscow correspondent, who deliberately lied about the [Ukrainian] famine to shield Stalin

Postscript

from Western accountability," and the false reporting of Hannah-Jones, the *New York Times'* Pulitzer-winning race correspondent, who deliberately lies about American history.[3]

As I write this, Arkansas senator Tom Cotton has proposed legislation that would prohibit federal money from going to schools that teach the 1619 Project. I am not clear that such a measure would pass constitutional muster, and it seems out of the question that it would pass in the Democrat-controlled House of Representatives, but it is a welcome sign that a US senator has recognized the existential threat posed by the 1619 curriculum. Perhaps Cotton's bill can be taken as the first stirring of a national debate that is long overdue.

Plainly my apprehension back in January 2020 – that interest in the 1619 Project would run out before I could publish the book – has been put to rest. The topic will be with us, I fear, for a long time to come.

I am grateful to Roger for proposing the idea, and I would like to thank several others for their generous help. Robert Paquette, emeritus professor of history at Hamilton College and an expert on antebellum slavery, read and critiqued the manuscript in fine detail. Likewise, my friend and fellow anthropologist Stanley Kurtz stopped my argument from wandering in crucial areas and made sure I didn't overlook important points. My NAS colleague, historian David Randall, helped me navigate the scholarly literature of a discipline that differs in many ways from my own. My good friend and Lincoln expert Tom Klingenstein helped me through the intricacies of Lincoln's views on race and colonization. Jessica Hornik Evans, my copyeditor at Encounter, did outstanding work in keeping my sometimes complicated syntax and meta-

Postscript

phoric license under control. I had help from several others who prefer to remain unnamed.

And I dedicate this book gratefully to my wife, Jody, who kept me organized and focused in the midst of the pandemic and the panic that gripped our city.

NOTES

Preliminaries

1   Jake Silverstein, "1619," *The New York Times Magazine*, August 18, 2019,
     4–5. Online version, "Why We Published The 1619 Project," Decem-
     ber 20, 2019, https://www.nytimes.com/interactive/2019/12/20/
     magazine/1619-intro.html.

Preface

1   Bartolomé de las Casas, *Memorial de remedios para las Indias* (1516); *A Short
     Account of the Destruction of the Indies* (1542); *History of the Indies* (1561, first
     printed 1875).
2   The New Laws of the Indies, 1542, Modern History Sourcebook,
     Fordham University, https://sourcebooks.fordham.edu/mod/1542new
     lawsindies.asp.
3   Cover text, and Silverstein, "Why We Published The 1619 Project,"
     https://www.nytimes.com/interactive/2019/08/14/magazine/1619-
     america-slavery.html.
4   John R. Jewitt, *White Slaves of Maquinna: John R. Jewitt's Narrative of Cap-
     ture and Confinement at Nootka* (1815; Surrey, BC, Canada: Heritage
     House, 2000).

Chapter 1

1   Rebecca Fraser, *The Mayflower: The Families, the Voyage, and the Founding of
     America* (New York: St. Martin's, 2017), 55.

Chapter 2

1   The paragraph comes from a letter John Rolfe wrote to Sir Edwin
     Sandys that is preserved at Magdalene College, Cambridge. The letter
     is reproduced in Susan M. Kingsbury, ed., *Records of the Virginia Company
     of London*, 3:243 (Washington, DC: Government Printing Office, 1933),
     https://www.loc.gov/resource/mtj8.vc03/?sp=267.
2   Quoted in Martha W. McCartney, *A Study of the Africans and African
     Americans on Jamestown Island and at Green Spring, 1619–1803* (National

Notes

Park Service and Colonial Williamsburg Foundation, 2003), 30, citing Kingsbury, *Records of the Virginia Company of London*, 3:93. The proclamation in its entirety says: "Every person to go to Church Sundays & holidaies or lye neck & heels on the Corps du Guard ye night following & be a slave ye week following 2d offence a month 3d a year & a day. 10. May 1618."

3   McCartney, *A Study of the Africans and African Americans on Jamestown Island and at Green Spring*, 1: "One of the project's principal goals was to chart the course of Africans and African Americans in the transition from servitude to slavery."

4   Alden T. Vaughan, "The Origins Debate: Slavery and Racism in Seventeenth-Century Virginia," *Virginia Magazine of History and Biography* 97, no. 3 (1989): 311–54, as referred to by McCartney, *A Study of the Africans and African Americans on Jamestown Island and at Green Spring*, 9.

5   Tim Hashaw, *The Birth of Black America: The First African Americans and the Pursuit of Freedom at Jamestown* (New York: Carroll & Graf, 2007), xvii.

6   See James Horn, "First Africans," in *1619: Jamestown and the Forging of American Democracy* (New York: Basic Books, 2018).

7   Horn, "First Africans," 98, 104.

8   Ira Berlin, *Many Thousands Gone: The First Two Centuries of Slavery in North America* (Cambridge, MA: Belknap Press of Harvard University Press, 1998), 29–32.

9   Silverstein, "Why We Published The 1619 Project," https://www.nytimes.com/interactive/2019/08/14/magazine/1619-america-slavery.html.

10   Silverstein, "We Respond to the Historians Who Critiqued The 1619 Project," *New York Times Magazine*, December 29, 2019, 6; online version, December 20, 2019, updated January 4, 2020, https://www.nytimes.com/2019/12/20/magazine/we-respond-to-the-historians-who-critiqued-the-1619-project.html.

11   "11 Facts About Human Trafficking," DoSomething.org, https://www.dosomething.org/us/facts/11-facts-about-human-trafficking.

12   James D. Graham, "The Slave Trade, Depopulation and Human Sacrifice in Benin History," *Cahiers d'Études africaines* 5, no. 18 (1965): 317–34.

13   Berlin, *Many Thousands Gone*, 44.

14   Berlin, *Many Thousands Gone*, 32.

15   Horn, *1619: Jamestown and the Forging of American Democracy*, 103, 108–9.

Notes

16   Nikole Hannah-Jones, "The Idea of America," *The New York Times Magazine*, August 18, 2019, 16; online version, "Our Democracy's Founding Ideals Were False When They Were Written: Black Americans Have Fought to Make Them True," August 14, 2019, https://www.nytimes.com/interactive/2019/08/14/magazine/black-history-american-democracy.html.

17   Henry Louis Gates Jr., "How Many Slaves Landed in the U.S.?" *100 Amazing Facts about the Negro*, https://www.pbs.org/wnet/african-americans-many-rivers-to-cross/history/how-many-slaves-landed-in-the-us/. The estimate of 12.5 million Africans sold into New World slavery comes from the Trans-Atlantic Slave Trade Database, housed by Harvard's Hutchins Center for African and African American Research and directed by David Eltis, https://hutchinscenter.fas.harvard.edu/trans-atlantic-slave-trade-database.

18   Horn, *1619: Jamestown and the Forging of American Democracy*, 67.

19   Horn, *1619: Jamestown and the Forging of American Democracy*, 63.

20   Horn, *1619: Jamestown and the Forging of American Democracy*, 63–64.

21   Daniel Webster, "Plymouth Oration," December 22, 1820, https://www.dartmouth.edu/~dwebster/speeches/plymouth-oration.html.

CHAPTER 3

1   Sara Jerde, "Janelle Monáe Narrates New York Times Ad for The 1619 Project," *Adweek*, February 5, 2020, https://www.adweek.com/tv-video/janelle-monae-narrates-new-york-times-ad-for-the-1619-project/.

2   Alexander Russo, "Nikole Hannah-Jones, the Beyoncé of Journalism," *Phi Delta Kappan*, October 12, 2017, https://kappanonline.org/russo-the-beyonce-of-journalism/; Nikole Hannah-Jones, "Segregation Now," *ProPublica*, April 16, 2014, https://www.propublica.org/article/segregation-now-full-text; "Choosing a School for My Daughter in a Segregated City," *The New York Times Magazine*, June 9, 2016, https://www.nytimes.com/2016/06/12/magazine/choosing-a-school-for-my-daughter-in-a-segregated-city.html; "The Problem We All Live With," *This American Life*, part 1, July 31, https://www.thisamericanlife.org/562/the-problem-we-all-live-with-part-one, and part 2, August 7, 2016, https://www.thisamericanlife.org/563/the-problem-we-all-live-with-part-two.

3   Jon Allsop, "Unpacking *The New York Times*'s Multitudes," *Columbia Journalism Review*, August 21, 2019, https://www.cjr.org/the_media_today/new-york-times-racism.php.

Notes

4   Nikole Hannah-Jones, Lavin Agency, https://www.thelavinagency.com/speakers/nikole-hannah-jones.

5   Hannah-Jones, speech at the University of Chicago Institute of Politics, October 7, 2019, https://www.youtube.com/watch?v=QwvyRSJ LoYU; "The 400 Year Legacy, with Nikole Hannah-Jones," *Why Is This Happening? with Chris Hayes* (podcast), November 12, 2019, https://www.stitcher.com/podcast/msnbc/why-is-this-happening/e/65377076; "I Live in a Slaveocracy," *The Touré Show* (podcast), January 8, 2020, https://podbay.fm/podcast/1313077481/e/1578470580.

6   Hannah-Jones, speech at the University of Chicago Institute of Politics.

7   Eric London, "Audio Recording Refutes Hannah-Jones' Claim That She Was Falsely Quoted by the World Socialist Web Site," November 27, 2019, https://www.wsws.org/en/articles/2019/11/27/hann-n27.html.

8   Mark Hemingway, "The New York Times Goes All In on Flawed 1619 Project," *RealClearPolitics*, February 21, 2020, https://www.realclearpolitics.com/articles/2020/02/21/new_york_times_goes_all_in_on_flawed_1619_project_142458.html.

9   Rich Lowry, "The Flagrant Distortions and Subtle Lies of the '1619 Project,'" *National Review*, October 7, 2019, https://www.nationalreview.com/2019/10/new-york-times-1619-project-distorts-history-of-slavery/.

10   Jeff Barrus, "Nikole Hannah-Jones Wins Pulitzer Prize for 1619 Project," Pulitzer Center, May 4, 2020, https://pulitzercenter.org/blog/nikole-hannah-jones-wins-pulitzer-prize-1619-project.

11   Charles Kesler, "Call Them the 1619 Riots," *New York Post*, June 19, 2020, https://nypost.com/2020/06/19/call-them-the-1619-riots/.

12   Allison Schuster, "Nikole Hannah-Jones Endorses Riots and Toppling Statues as a Product of the 1619 Project," *The Federalist*, June 20, 2020, https://thefederalist.com/2020/06/20/nikole-hannah-jones-endorses-riots-and-toppling-statues-as-a-product-of-the-1619-project/.

13   Amanda N'Duka, "Lionsgate, Oprah Winfrey Team with Pulitzer Prize Winner Nikole Hannah-Jones to Develop 'The 1619 Project' for Multiple Platforms," *Deadline*, July 8, 2020, https://deadline.com/2020/07/lionsgate-oprah-winfrey-nikole-hannah-jones-the-1619-project-1202980325/amp/.

Notes

CHAPTER 4

1   Nikole Hannah-Jones, transcribed portion of panel discussion, "The 1619 Project," *Karen Hunter Show* town hall, December 19, 2019, https://www.youtube.com/watch?v=IF36IQH3BRw (from 17:55 to 18:35).

2   American Council of Trustees and Alumni, "Losing America's Memory: Historical Illiteracy in the 21st Century," February 16, 2000, https://www.goacta.org/images/download/losing_americas_memory.pdf. ACTA followed this original study with other studies showing that the level of historical literacy has declined still further since 2000.

3   Ilya Somin, "Public Ignorance about the Constitution," *Washington Post*, September 15, 2017, https://www.washingtonpost.com/news/volokh-conspiracy/wp/2017/09/15/public-ignorance-about-the-constitution/. Somin cites data from a survey by the University of Pennsylvania's Annenberg Public Policy Center.

4   Nation's Report Card, "How Did U.S. Students Score on the Most Recent Assessments?," 2018 assessment, https://www.nationsreportcard.gov/.

5   Wesley Morris, "For Centuries Black Music, Forged in Bondage, Has Been the Sound of Complete Artistic Freedom – No Wonder Everybody Is Always Stealing It," *The New York Times Magazine*, August 18, 2019; online version, https://www.nytimes.com/interactive/2019/08/14/magazine/music-black-culture-appropriation.html.

6   Hannah-Jones, "The Idea of America"; online version, "Our Democracy's Founding Ideals Were False When They Were Written" (this and subsequent Hannah-Jones quotes in this chapter).

7   Leslie M. Harris, "I Helped Fact-Check the 1619 Project: The *Times* Ignored Me," *Politico*, March 6, 2020, https://www.politico.com/news/magazine/2020/03/06/1619-project-new-york-times-mistake-122248.

8   Harris, "I Helped Fact-Check the 1619 Project."

9   Harris, "I Helped Fact-Check the 1619 Project."

CHAPTER 5

1   Sean Wilentz, "American Slavery and 'the Relentless Unforeseen,'" *New York Review of Books*, November 19, 2019, https://www.nybooks.com/daily/2019/11/19/american-slavery-and-the-relentless-unforeseen/.

2   Wilentz, "American Slavery and 'the Relentless Unforeseen.'"

3   Wilentz, "American Slavery and 'the Relentless Unforeseen.'"

Notes

4   Hannah-Jones, "The Idea of America," 17; online version, "Our Democracy's Founding Ideals Were False When They Were Written."

5   Hannah-Jones, "The Idea of America," 18; online version, "Our Democracy's Founding Ideals Were False When They Were Written."

6   Wilentz, "American Slavery and 'the Relentless Unforeseen.'"

7   Wilentz, "American Slavery and 'the Relentless Unforeseen.'"

8   Sean Wilentz, "A Matter of Facts," *The Atlantic*, January 22, 2020, https://www.theatlantic.com/ideas/archive/2020/01/1619-project-new-york-times-wilentz/605152/.

9   Tom Mackaman, "An Interview with Historian Gordon Wood on the New York Times' 1619 Project," World Social Web Site, November 28, 2019, https://www.wsws.org/en/articles/2019/11/28/wood-n28.html.

10   Mackaman, "An Interview with Historian Gordon Wood."

11   Mackaman, "An Interview with Historian Gordon Wood."

12   Victoria Bynum, James M. McPherson, James Oakes, Sean Wilentz, and Gordon S. Wood, Letter to the Editor, *New York Times*, December 20, 2019, https://www.nytimes.com/2019/12/20/magazine/we-respond-to-the-historians-who-critiqued-the-1619-project.html.

13   Silverstein, "We Respond to the Historians Who Critiqued the 1619 Project."

14   Jill Lepore, *These Truths: A History of the United States* (New York: Norton, 2018), 94.

15   Gordon Wood, "Historian Gordon Wood Responds to the New York Times' Defense of the 1619 Project," *World Socialist Web Site*, December 24, 2019, https://www.wsws.org/en/articles/2019/12/24/nytr-d24.html.

16   Gordon S. Wood, "'1774' Review: The Year That Changed the World," *Wall Street Journal*, February 21, 2020, https://www.wsj.com/articles/1774-review-the-year-that-changed-the-world-11582303285.

17   Silverstein, "An Update to The 1619 Project," *New York Times*, March 11, 2020, https://www.nytimes.com/2020/03/11/magazine/an-update-to-the-1619-project.html.

18   Silverstein, "An Update to The 1619 Project."

19   Silverstein, "An Update to The 1619 Project."

20   Alan Taylor, *The Internal Enemy: Slavery and War in Virginia, 1772–1832* (New York: Norton, 2013), 21.

21   George William Van Cleve, *A Slaveholders' Union: Slavery, Politics, and the Constitution in the Early American Republic* (Chicago: University of Chicago Press, 2010), 37, 38, 40.

Notes

22 Seymour Drescher, *Abolition: A History of Slavery and Antislavery* (Cambridge: Cambridge University Press, 2009), 120.

23 Christopher Leslie Brown, *Moral Capital: Foundations of British Abolitionism* (Chapel Hill: University of North Carolina Press, 2006), 110.

24 Taylor, *The Internal Enemy*, 22.

25 Quoted in Taylor, *The Internal Enemy*, 21.

26 Wood, "Historian Gordon Wood Responds to the New York Times' Defense of the 1619 Project."

27 Wilentz, "A Matter of Facts."

28 Van Cleve, *A Slaveholders' Union*, 33, 36, 37.

29 Van Cleve, *A Slaveholders' Union*, 35; chap. 1, n86, 304.

30 "Twelve Scholars Critique the 1619 Project and the New York Times Magazine Editor Responds," *History News Network*, Columbian College of Arts and Sciences, George Washington University, December 30, 2019, and January 10, 2020, https://hnn.us/article/174140.

CHAPTER 6

1 Joseph A. Wulfsohn, "NYT Magazine Reporter Suggests Destroying Property 'Is Not Violence,'" Fox News, June 3, 2020, https://www.foxnews.com/media/nyt-magazine-nikole-hannah-jones-destroying-property-not-violence.

2 Nikole Hannah-Jones, interview with Christiane Amanpour, *Amanpour & Co.*, PBS, June 1, 2020, http://www.pbs.org/wnet/amanpour-and-company/video/how-americas-history-racism-informs-current-moment-zj5six-2/. For King's speech, see the American Psychological Association, "King's Challenge to the Nation's Social Scientists," https://www.apa.org/monitor/features/king-challenge.

3 Gennette Cordova, "Destruction Caused by White Rioters Is Being Widely Acknowledged, but Are There Ulterior Motives?" *Revolt*, June 2, 2020, https://www.revolt.tv/2020/6/2/21278508/white-rioters-looters-protests-review; Alexander Mallin, "Evidence That Antifa, 'Foreign Actors' Involved in Sowing Unrest and Violence: AG Barr," ABC News, June 4, 2020, https://abcnews.go.com/Politics/ag-barr-evidence-antifa-foreign-actors-involved-sowing/story?id=71066996.

4 Kesler, "Call Them the 1619 Riots"; Schuster, "Nikole Hannah-Jones Endorses Riots and Toppling Statues as a Product of the 1619 Project."

5 Jennifer Schuessler, "Ibram X. Kendi Has a Cure for America's 'Metastatic Racism,'" *New York Times*, August 6, 2019, https://www.nytimes.com/2019/08/06/arts/ibram-x-kendi-antiracism.html.

Notes

6   Jeffrey C. Stewart, "Fighting Racism Even, and Especially, Where We Don't Realize It Exists," *New York Times*, August 20, 2019, https://www.nytimes.com/2019/08/20/books/review/how-to-be-an-anti racist-ibram-x-kendi.html.

7   "Examining Slavery's Legacy with Nikole Hannah-Jones and Ibram X. Kendi," *Why Is This Happening? with Chris Hayes*, December 6, 2019, https://www.nbcnews.com/think/opinion/examining-slavery-s-legacy-nikole-hannah-jones-ibram-x-kendi-ncna1085646.

8   "The 1619 Project Resource Page," *EdJustice*, National Education Association, https://neaedjustice.org/the-1619-project-resource-page/.

9   "Black Lives Matter at School Week of Action Curriculum Fair," D.C. Area Educators for Social Change, https://www.dcareaeducators4 socialjustice.org/events/black-lives-matter-at-school-week-of-action-curriculum-fair-4n9b6.

10   "Teaching with New York Times 1619 Project," Zinn Education Project, https://www.zinnedproject.org/news/teaching-1619-project/.

11   "History," Teaching for Change, https://www.teachingforchange.org/about/history.

12   "Zinn Education Project," Teaching for Change, https://www.teach-ingforchange.org/contact/zinn-education-project.

13   "History," Rethinking Schools, https://www.rethinkingschools.org/about-us/history.

14   Adam Sanchez, "Introduction," *Teaching a People's History of Abolition and the Civil War* (Rethinking Schools, 2019), Zinn Education Project, https://www.zinnedproject.org/materials/teaching-peoples-history-of-abolition.

15   Hannah-Jones, "The Idea of America," 20.

16   Milwaukee Black Lives Matter at School, MTEAching All Children, https://mtea.weac.org/?s=1619.

17   "Black History Month," California Teachers Association, https://www.cta.org/events/awareness-events/black-history-month.

18   "Connecting Educators Reception: Your Introduction to Resources on the 1619 Project and 'The Weekly,'" Pulitzer Center, https://pulitzer-center.org/event/connecting-educators-reception-your-intro duction-resources-1619-project-and-weekly.

19   Katie Brown, "On Tour with Nikole Hannah-Jones, in Chicago and North Carolina," Pulitzer Center, October 14, 2019, https://pulitzer-center.org/blog/tour-nikole-hannah-jones-chicago-and-north-carolina.

Notes

20 Meerabelle Jesuthasan, "The 1619 Project Sparks Dialogue and Reflection in Schools Nationwide," Pulitzer Center, December 20, 2019, https://pulitzercenter.org/blog/1619-project-sparks-dialogue-and-reflection-schools-nationwide.

21 "The 1619 Project Curriculum," Pulitzer Center, https://pulitzer-center.org/lesson-plan-grouping/1619-project-curriculum.

22 Mark Schulte, "Journalism as a Textbook: Pulitzer Center and the 1619 Project," ShareMyLesson, January 29, 2020, https://sharemyl-esson.com/blog/1619-project.

23 Schulte, "Journalism as a Textbook."

24 Southern Poverty Law Center, "Teaching Hard History: American Slavery," 2018, https://www.splcenter.org/sites/default/files/tt_hard_history_american_slavery.pdf.

25 Southern Poverty Law Center, Teaching Hard History, https://www.splcenter.org/20180131/teaching-hard-history.

26 Brad Bennett, "Maryland Teacher Incorporates Hard Lessons about Slavery into Public School Curriculum," Southern Poverty Law Center, August 20, 2019, https://www.splcenter.org/news/2019/08/20/maryland-teacher-incorporates-hard-lessons-about-slavery-public-school-curriculum.

27 "The SPLC's 'Teaching Tolerance': What Parents, Teachers, and Administrators Need to Know," Family Research Council (2019), 22, https://downloads.frc.org/EF/EF19J06.pdf.

CHAPTER 7

1 Eugene Aubrey Stratton, *Plymouth Colony, Its History & People, 1620–1691* (Salt Lake City: Ancestry Publishing, 1986).

2 Stratton, *Plymouth Colony, Its History & People*, 29.

3 H. Roger King, *Cape Cod and Plymouth Colony in the Seventeenth Century* (Lanham, MD: University Press of America, 1993), 171.

4 Walter A. McDougall, *Freedom Just Around the Corner: A New American History 1585–1828* (New York: HarperCollins, 2004), 54.

5 William Bradford, *Of Plymouth Plantation*, Early Americas Digital Archive, http://eada.lib.umd.edu/text-entries/of-plymouth-plantation/. (Original source: *Bradford's History of Plymouth Plantation, 1606–1646*, ed. William T. Davis [New York: Scribner's, 1908].)

6 See, e.g., George D. Langdon Jr., "The Franchise and Political Democracy in Plymouth Colony," *William and Mary Quarterly* 20, no. 4 (1963): 513–26; Nathaniel B. Shurtleff, et al., *Records of New Plymouth* (1620–

Notes

1693), 12 vols. (Boston: Press of W. White, 1855–61); Alexander Young, *Chronicles of the Pilgrim Fathers of the Colony of Plymouth, from 1602 to 1625* (1844; Boston: New England Historic Genealogical Society, 2016); Samuel Eliot Morison, *The Story of the "Old Colony" of New Plymouth, 1620–1692* (New York: Knopf, 1956).

CHAPTER 8

1   Walter Johnson, *River of Darkness: Slavery and Empire in the Cotton Kingdom* (Cambridge, MA: Belknap Press of Harvard University Press, 2013); Sven Beckert, *Empire of Cotton: A Global History* (New York: Vintage, 2014); Edward E. Baptist, *The Half Has Never Been Told: Slavery and the Making of American Capitalism* (New York: Basic, 2014).

2   Baptist, *The Half Has Never Been Told*, 3.

3   Sven Beckert and Seth Rockman, eds., *Slavery's Capitalism: A New History of American Economic Development* (Philadelphia: University of Pennsylvania Press, 2016).

4   Johnson, *River of Darkness*, 5, 11, 80–81, 97–98.

5   Alan L. Olmstead and Paul W. Rhode, "Cotton, Slavery, and the New History of Capitalism," *Explorations in Economic History* 67 (January 2018): 1.

6   Matthew Desmond, "In Order to Understand the Brutality of American Capitalism, You Have to Start on the Plantation," *The New York Times Magazine*, August 18, 2019, 30–40; online version, https://www.nytimes.com/interactive/2019/08/14/magazine/slavery-capitalism.html.

7   Desmond, "In Order to Understand the Brutality of American Capitalism, You Have to Start on the Plantation."

8   Desmond, "In Order to Understand the Brutality of American Capitalism, You Have to Start on the Plantation."

9   Desmond, "In Order to Understand the Brutality of American Capitalism, You Have to Start on the Plantation."

10   Desmond, "In Order to Understand the Brutality of American Capitalism, You Have to Start on the Plantation."

11   W. B. Allen, "The New York Times Resurrects the Positive Good Slavery Argument," *Law & Liberty*, October 2, 2019, https://www.lawliberty.org/2019/10/02/the-new-york-times-resurrects-the-positive-good-slavery-argument/.

12   Desmond draws on his 2016 book *Evicted: Poverty and Profit in the American City* (New York: Crown, 2016) for a portion of his argument in his 1619

Notes

essay, where he decries the use of home mortgages as a financial instrument in securing housing. *Evicted* deals with people reduced to living in trailer parks outside Milwaukee.

13 Allen, "The New York Times Resurrects the Positive Good Slavery Argument."

14 Robert Paquette, personal communication with the author, April 1, 2020.

15 Alexis de Tocqueville, *Democracy in America*, trans. Gerald Bevan (London: Penguin, 2003), 405–8.

16 Ta-Nehisi Coates, "Talk to Me Like I'm Stupid: Tocqueville in the South," *Atlantic*, May 4, 2012, https://www.theatlantic.com/personal/archive/2012/05/talk-to-me-like-im-stupid-tocqueville-in-the-south/256736/.

17 Deirdre McCloskey, "Slavery Did Not Make America Rich," *Reason*, August/September 2018, https://reason.com/2018/07/19/slavery-did-not-make-america-r/.

18 John Clegg, "How Slavery Shaped American Capitalism," *Jacobin*, August 28, 2019, https://jacobinmag.com/2019/08/how-slavery-shaped-american-capitalism.

19 William L. Anderson, "The *New York Times* Gets Slavery (and Capitalism) Wrong, Yet Again," *Mises Wire*, Mises Institute, August 31, 2019, https://mises.org/wire/new-york-times-gets-slavery-and-capitalism-wrong-yet-again.

20 Robert William Fogel, *Without Consent or Contract: The Rise and Fall of American Slavery* (New York: Norton, 1989), 96–102.

21 Anderson, "The *New York Times* Gets Slavery (and Capitalism) Wrong, Yet Again."

22 Hans Eicholz, "Slavery Gave Us Double-Entry Bookkeeping?" *Law & Liberty*, October 2, 2019, https://www.lawliberty.org/2019/10/02/slavery-gave-us-double-entry-bookkeeping/.

23 John Phelan, "What the 1619 Project Gets Wrong about Slavery and Economics," Foundation for Economic Education, September 15, 2019, https://fee.org/articles/what-the-1619-project-gets-wrong-about-slavery-and-economics/.

24 Phelan, "What the 1619 Project Gets Wrong about Slavery and Economics."

25 Robert L. Paquette, "Capitalism and Forced Labor," review of Edward E. Baptist's *The Half Has Never Been Told*, *Law & Liberty*, March 21, 2016, https://lawliberty.org/book-review/capitalism-and-forced-labor/.

26 Phillip W. Magness, "The Statistical Errors of the Reparations Agenda,"

Notes

American Institute for Economic Research, June 23, 2019, https://www.aier. org/article/the-statistical-errors-of-the-reparations-agenda/.

27   Magness paraphrases Olmstead and Rhode, who write: "By adding the value of inputs used to produce cotton, Baptist double counts costs already subsumed in the cotton's price." And: "But then, with the help of atrocious national product accounting procedures, he boosts cotton's 'role' to more than $600 million[,] 'almost half of the economic activity of the United States in 1836.'" Olmstead and Rhode, "Cotton, Slavery, and the New History of Capitalism," 13 (quoting Baptist, 321–22).

28   Olmstead and Rhode, "Cotton, Slavery, and the New History of Capitalism," 8, 9.

29   Magness, "The Statistical Errors of the Reparations Agenda," quoting Carol Anderson, *White Rage: The Unspoken Truth of Our Racial Divide* (New York: Bloomsbury USA, 2016), 11.

30   Paquette, "Capitalism and Forced Labor."

31   Robert William Fogel and Stanley L. Engerman, *Time on the Cross: The Economics of American Negro Slavery* (Boston: Little, Brown, 1974).

32   Paquette, "Capitalism and Forced Labor."

33   Trevor Burnard, "'The Righteous Will Shine Like the Sun': Writing an Evocative History of Antebellum American Slavery," *Slavery & Abolition* 36, no. 1 (2015): 180.

34   Stanley L. Engerman, "Review of *The Business of Slavery and the Rise of American Capitalism, 1815–1860* by Calvin Schermerhorn and *The Half Has Never Been Told: Slavery and the Making of American Capitalism* by Edward E. Baptist," *Journal of Economic Literature* 55, no. 2 (2017): 637–43, https://www.aeaweb.org/articles?id=10.1257/jel.20151334.

35   Phillip W. Magness, "A Comment on the 'New' History of American Capitalism," August 17, 2019, https://ssrn.com/abstract=3438828, quoting James Henry Hammond, *Plantation Manual, 1857–58*, Hammond Collection, University of South Carolina Library, http://www. scpronet.com/modjeskaschool/wp-content/uploads/2017/03/ James-Henry-Hammond-Plantation-Manual.pdf.

36   Phillip W. Magness, "How the 1619 Project Rehabilitates the 'King Cotton' Thesis," *National Review,* August 26, 2019, https://www. nationalreview.com/2019/08/1619-project-new-york-times-king-cotton-thesis/.

37   Phillip W. Magness, "Fact Checking the 1619 Project and Its Critics," *American Institute for Economic Research,* December 23, 2019, https://

www.aier.org/article/fact-checking-the-1619-project-and-its-critics/.

38 Phillip W. Magness, "The 1619 Project Debate: A Bibliography," *American Institute for Economic Research*, January 3, 2020, https://www.aier.org/article/the-1619-project-debate-a-bibliography/.

39 Phillip W. Magness, "The Case for Retracting Matthew Desmond's 1619 Project Essay," *American Institute for Economic Research*, February 11, 2020, https://www.aier.org/article/the-case-for-retracting-matthew-desmonds-1619-project-essay/.

40 Phillip W. Magness, "The 1619 Project: An Epitaph," *American Institute for Economic Research*, March 16, 2020, https://www.aier.org/article/the-1619-project-an-epitaph/. NB: In April 2020, Magness published *The 1619 Project: A Critique* (American Institute for Economic Research), which gathers in one place his previously published essays on the 1619 Project.

CHAPTER 9

1 Abraham Lincoln, "Address on Colonization to a Deputation of Negroes," August 14, 1862, in *Collected Works of Abraham Lincoln*, ed. Roy P. Basler (New Brunswick, NJ: Rutgers University Press, 1953), 5:371. Digital edition, University of Michigan Digital Library Production Service, https://quod.lib.umich.edu/l/lincoln/lincoln5/1:812?rgn=div1;view=fulltext.

2 Lincoln, Speech at Peoria, Illinois, October 16, 1854, in *Collected Works of Abraham Lincoln*, 2:248, https://quod.lib.umich.edu/l/lincoln/lincoln2/1:282?rgn=div1;sort=occur;subview=detail;type=simple;view=fulltext;q1=selfishness.

3 Lewis E. Lehrman, *Lincoln at Peoria: The Turning Point* (Mechanicsburg, PA: Stackpole Books, 2008), 315 (text of the speech), 217–18.

4 Lincoln, "Address on Colonization," *Collected Works of Abraham Lincoln*, 5:372.

5 Kate Masur, "The African American Delegation to Abraham Lincoln: A Reappraisal," *Civil War History* 56, no. 2 (2010), 119, 130, http://housedivided.dickinson.edu/sites/emancipation/files/2012/07/Masur-article.pdf.

6 Hannah-Jones, "The Idea of America"; online version, "Our Democracy's Founding Ideals Were False When They Were Written."

7 Masur, "The African American Delegation to Abraham Lincoln," 120.

8 Hannah-Jones, "The Idea of America"; online version, "Our Democracy's Founding Ideals Were False When They Were Written."

Notes

9   Sidney Blumenthal, "The Emergence of Abraham Lincoln," *Washington Monthly*, December 9, 2019, https://washingtonmonthly.com/2019/12/09/abraham-lincolns-political-emergence/.

10 James M. McPherson, "Lincoln the Devil" (review of Lerone Bennett Jr.'s *Forced into Glory: Abraham Lincoln's White Dream*), *New York Times*, August 27, 2000, https://www.nytimes.com/2000/08/27/books/lincoln-the-devil.html.

11 Eric Foner, Review of *Forced into Glory: Abraham Lincoln's White Dream*, by Lerone Bennett Jr., *Los Angeles Times Book Review*, April 9, 2000, http://www.ericfoner.com/reviews/040900latimes.html. See also John M. Barr, "Holding Up a Flawed Mirror to the American Soul: Abraham Lincoln in the Writings of Lerone Bennett Jr.," *Journal of the Abraham Lincoln Association* 35 (winter 2014): 43–65.

12 Thomasi McDonald, "Americans Pretend Racism Is a Relic: UNC Alum Nikole Hannah-Jones, Who Envisioned the NYT's 1619 Project, Says It's Time to Stop Hiding from Our Sins," *Indy Week*, August 27, 2019, https://indyweek.com/news/northcarolina/nikole-hannah-jones-1619-project/.

13 Tom Mackaman. "An Interview with Historian James Oakes on the New York Times' 1619 Project," *World Socialist Web Site*, November 18, 2019, https://www.wsws.org/en/articles/2019/11/18/oake-n18.html.

14 Lincoln to Horace Greeley, August 22, 1862, *Collected Works of Abraham Lincoln*, 5:388, https://quod.lib.umich.edu/l/lincoln/lincoln5/1:848?rgn=div1;view=fulltext.

15 Mackaman, "An Interview with Historian James Oakes."

16 Tom Mackaman, "An Interview with Historian James McPherson on the New York Times' 1619 Project," *World Socialist Web Site*, November 14, 2019, https://www.wsws.org/en/articles/2019/11/14/mcph-n14html.

17 Tom Mackaman, "An Interview with Historian Richard Carwardine on the New York Times' 1619 Project," *World Socialist Web Site*, December 31, 2019, https://www.wsws.org/en/articles/2019/12/31/carw-d31.html.

18 Mackaman, "An Interview with Historian Richard Carwardine."

19 Wilentz, "A Matter of Facts."

20 Wilentz, "A Matter of Facts."

21 Lincoln, "Eulogy on Henry Clay," July 6, 1852, *Collected Works of Abraham Lincoln*, 2:132, https://quod.lib.umich.edu/l/lincoln/lincoln2/1:193?rgn=div1;singlegenre=All;sort=occur;subview=detail;type=simple;view=fulltext;q1=eulogy+on+henry+clay.

Notes

22 Allen C. Guelzo, "Preaching a Conspiracy Theory," *City Journal*, December 8, 2019, https://www.city-journal.org/1619-project-conspiracy-theory.

23 Allen C. Guelzo, "The 1619 Project's Outrageous, Lying Slander of Abe Lincoln," *New York Post*, March 3, 2020, https://nypost.com/2020/03/03/the-1619-projects-outrageous-lying-slander-of-abe-lincoln/.

24 Michael Burlingame, *Abraham Lincoln: A Life* (Baltimore: Johns Hopkins University Press, 2008), 2:3052.

25 Michael Vorenberg, "Abraham Lincoln and the Politics of Black Colonization," *Journal of the Abraham Lincoln Association* 14, no. 2 (1993): 22–45, http://hdl.handle.net/2027/spo.2629860.0014.204.

26 Vorenberg, "Abraham Lincoln and the Politics of Black Colonization."

27 Vorenberg, "Abraham Lincoln and the Politics of Black Colonization."

28 Phillip Shaw Paludan, "Lincoln and Colonization: Policy or Propaganda?" *Journal of the Abraham Lincoln Association* 25, no. 1 (2004): 23–37, http://hdl.handle.net/2027/spo.2629860.0025.104.

CHAPTER 10

1 See Natalie Mears, "Public Worship and Political Participation in Elizabethan England," *Journal of British Studies* 51, no. 1 (2012), DOI: https://doi.org/10.1086/662297.

2 "A Letter Sent from New England to a friend in these parts, setting forth a brief and true Declaration of the worth of that Plantation; As also certain useful Directions for such as intend a Voyage into those Parts," *Mourt's Relation: A Journal of the Pilgrims at Plymouth, 1622*, part 6, Plymouth Colony Archive Project, http://www.histarch.illinois.edu/plymouth/mourt6.html.

3 William Bradford, *Bradford's History of the Plymouth Settlement, 1608–1650*, rendered into modern English by Harold Paget (New York: Dutton, 1920), 89.

4 "A Letter Sent from New England to a friend in these parts" (*Mourt's Relation*), Plymouth Colony Archive Project.

5 "A Letter Sent from New England to a friend in these parts" (*Mourt's Relation*), Plymouth Colony Archive Project.

6 Bradford, *Bradford's History of the Plymouth Settlement*, 89.

7 Bradford, *Bradford's History of the Plymouth Settlement*, 90.

8 Bradford, *Bradford's History of the Plymouth Settlement*, 93.

9 Hannah-Jones, "The 1619 Project," *Karen Hunter Show* town hall,

Notes

December 19, 2019, https://www.youtube.com/watch?v=IF36IQH3 BRw (from 1:32.03 to 1:32.07).

10 Darcel Rockett, "5 Minutes with Nikole Hannah-Jones, the Architect behind *The New York Times*' '1619 Project,'" *Chicago Tribune*, October 10, 2019, https://www.chicagotribune.com/lifestyles/ct-life-nikole-hannah-jones-1619-project-20191009-20191010-m3rym2hxyncj7ihc n67q2gekdq-story.html.

11 Nikole Hannah-Jones, "What Is Owed," *The New York Times Magazine*, June 30, 2020, https://www.nytimes.com/interactive/2020/06/24/magazine/reparations-slavery.html; see also Peter Wood, "The Poison of Reparations," *Spectator USA*, June 30, 2020, https://spectator.us/poison-reparations-slavery-1619-project/.

CHAPTER 11

1 Alex Lichtenstein, "1619 and All That," *American Historical Review* 125, no. 1 (2020): xv–xxi, https://academic.oup.com/ahr/article/125/1/xv/5714757; Alex Lichtenstein, "1619 and All That," *History News Network*, January 21, 2020, https://historynewsnetwork.org/article/174168.

2 Lichtenstein, "1619 and All That."

3 Lichtenstein, "1619 and All That."

4 Lichtenstein, "1619 and All That."

5 Lichtenstein, "1619 and All That."

6 Lichtenstein, "1619 and All That."

7 Victoria Bynum, "My Response to Alex Lichtenstein Regarding the 1619 Project," *World Socialist Web Site*, January 31, 2020, https://www.wsws.org/en/articles/2020/01/31/resp-j31.html.

8 David North and Tom Mackaman, "A Reply to the *American Historical Review*'s Defense of the 1619 Project," *World Socialist Web Site*, January 31, 2020, https://www.wsws.org/en/articles/2020/01/31/ahrr-j31.html.

9 North and Mackaman, "A Reply to the *American Historical Review*'s Defense of the 1619 Project."

CHAPTER 12

1 Herb Lubalin Study Center, "*The New York Times Magazine*, The 1619 Project issue 2019, online edition by *The New York Times*," *Fonts in Use*, November 25, 2019, https://fontsinuse.com/uses/29409/the-new-york-times-magazine-the-1619-project-.

Notes

2 Silverstein, "1619," 5 (online version, "Why We Published The 1619 Project").

3 "2019 Annual Report," *Pulitzer Center on Crisis Reporting*, https://pulitzercenter.org/blog/2019-pulitzer-center-annual-report.

4 Meerabelle Jesuthasan, "The 1619 Project Sparks Dialogue and Reflection in Schools Nationwide," Pulitzer Center, December 20, 2019, https://pulitzercenter.org/blog/1619-project-sparks-dialogue-and-reflection-schools-nationwide.

5 "Buffalo City School District at a Glance," *NYSED Data Site*, https://data.nysed.gov/profile.php?instid=800000052968; Matt Peterson, "CPS Enrollment Declines by 6,000 Students," *WTTW News*, November 8, 2019, https://news.wttw.com/2019/11/08/cps-enrollment-declines-6000-students; "DCPS Enrollment Increases in School Year 2018–2019," *District of Columbia Public Schools*, November 7, 2018, https://dcps.dc.gov/release/dcps-enrollment-increases-school-year-2018-2019; "Total School Districts, Student Enrollment by State and Metro Area," *Governing: The Future of States and Localities*, https://www.governing.com/gov-data/education-data/school-district-totals-average-enrollment-statistics-for-states-metro-areas.html.

6 Maya Riser-Kositsky, "Education Statistics: Facts about American Schools," *Education Week*, December 31, 2019, https://www.edweek.org/ew/issues/education-statistics/index.html.

7 Cynthia Greenlee, "How History Textbooks Reflect America's Refusal to Reckon with Slavery," *Vox*, August 26, 2019, https://www.vox.com/identities/2019/8/26/20829771/slavery-textbooks-history.

8 Greenlee, "How History Textbooks Reflect America's Refusal to Reckon with Slavery."

9 Mabel B. Casner and Ralph Henry Gabriel, *Exploring American History* (New York and Chicago: Harcourt, Brace, 1931), 398, 414.

10 Casner and Gabriel, *Exploring American History*, 433–34.

11 Casner and Gabriel, *Exploring American History*, 501–3.

12 Donald Yacovone, "Teaching White Supremacy: U.S. History Textbooks and the Influence of Historians," Houston Institute, March 6, 2018, https://medium.com/houstonmarshall/teaching-white-supremacy-u-s-history-textbooks-and-the-influence-of-historians-b614c5d2781b.

13 Joseph Moreau, *Schoolbook Nation: Conflicts over American History Textbooks from the Civil War to the Present* (Ann Arbor: University of Michigan Press, 2004), 272–73.

Notes

14 Joseph Moreau, "The American Textbook Wars: The Revised Edition," *History News Network*, May 23, 2005, http://hnn.us/articles/11778.html.

15 Moreau, "The American Textbook Wars."

16 Moreau, *Schoolbook Nation*, 273, 274.

17 Moreau, *Schoolbook Nation*, 274.

18 Moreau, *Schoolbook Nation*, 275, 276.

19 Moreau, *Schoolbook Nation*, 267–272.

20 Moreau, *Schoolbook Nation*, 277.

21 Moreau, *Schoolbook Nation*, 281.

22 Moreau, *Schoolbook Nation*, 283.

23 Moreau, *Schoolbook Nation*, 299, 300.

24 Moreau, *Schoolbook Nation*, 313, 328.

25 Moreau, *Schoolbook Nation*, 320.

26 Alvin Wolf, "Minorities in U.S. History Textbooks, 1945–1985," *The Clearing House* 65, no. 5 (1992): 297.

27 Kyle Ward, *History in the Making: An Absorbing Look at How American History Has Changed in the Telling over the Last 200 Years* (New York: New Press, 2006).

28 Robin Lindley, "Textbooks and History Standards: An Historical Overview," *History News Network*, December 17, 2013, https://historynewsnetwork.org/article/130766.

29 Lynne V. Cheney, "The End of History," *Wall Street Journal*, October 20, 1994, https://online.wsj.com/media/EndofHistory.pdf; Gary Nash, Charlotte Crabtree, and Ross E. Dunn, *History on Trial: Culture Wars and the Teaching of the Past* (New York: Vintage, 2000).

30 "Scholars Oppose New APUSH," National Association of Scholars, June 3, 2015, https://www.nas.org/blogs/press_release/scholars_oppose_new_apush.

31 Frances FitzGerald, *America Revised: History Schoolbooks in the Twentieth Century* (New York: Vintage, 1979), 90–94.

32 FitzGerald, *America Revised*, 39.

33 The series had two sequels, *Roots: The Next Generations* (1979) and *Roots: The Gift* (1988); a remake of *Roots* aired on the History channel in 2016.

34 Melinda D. Anderson, "What Kids Are Really Learning about Slavery," *The Atlantic*, February 1, 2018, https://www.theatlantic.com/education/archive/2018/02/what-kids-are-really-learning-about-slavery/552098/.

35 Anderson, "What Kids Are Really Learning about Slavery."

Notes

36 Thomas Jefferson, "The Anas," in *The Writings of Thomas Jefferson*, edited by H. A. Washington (1854; Cambridge: Cambridge University Press, 2011), 9:119.

37 Sean Wilentz, *No Property in Man: Slavery and Antislavery at the Nation's Founding*, 2nd ed. (Cambridge, MA: Harvard University Press, 2019), xiv.

38 Anderson, "What Kids Are Really Learning about Slavery."

39 Howard Zinn, *A People's History of the United States* (New York: Harper-Perennial, 2015), 178.

40 James A. Henretta, Eric Hinderaker, Rebecca Edwards, and Robert O. Self, *America's History*, 8th ed. (New York: St. Martin's, 2014).

41 Pulitzer Center Education, "Lesson Plan: Exploring 'The Idea of America' by Nikole Hannah-Jones," August 13, 2019, https://pulitzer center.org/builder/lesson/lesson-plan-exploring-idea-america-nikole-hannah-jones-26503.

42 Pulitzer Center Education, "Lesson Plan: Exploring 'The Idea of America' by Nikole Hannah-Jones."

CHAPTER 13

1 Maureen Balleza and Kate Zernike, "The 2004 Campaign: National Guard – Memos on Bush Are Fake but Accurate, Typist Says," *New York Times*, September 15, 2004, https://www.nytimes.com/2004/09/15/us/the-2004-campaign-national-guard-memos-on-bush-are-fake-but-accurate.html.

2 Leah Barkoukis, "AOC: Being Morally Right Is More Important Than Being Factually Correct," *Townhall*, January 7, 2019, https://townhall.com/tipsheet/leahbarkoukis/2019/01/07/aoc-it-doesnt-matter-if-im-factually-correct-about-things-n2538586.

3 "What's 'Fake News'? 60 Minutes Producers Investigate," *60 Minutes Overtime*, March 26, 2017, https://www.cbsnews.com/news/whats-fake-news-60-minutes-producers-investigate/.

4 Robert L. Woodson, "'The 1619 Project' Hurts Blacks," *Wall Street Journal*, August 28, 2019, https://www.wsj.com/articles/the-1619-project-hurts-blacks-11567033108.

5 "About the 1776 Unites Campaign," https://1776unites.com/.

6 Robert Woodson, "The Crucial Voice of 1776," *Washington Examiner*, February 13, 2020, https://www.washingtonexaminer.com/opinion/op-eds/the-crucial-voice-of-1776.

7 Adam Serwer, "The Fight Over the 1619 Project Is Not About the

Notes

Facts," *The Atlantic*, December 23, 2019, https://www.theatlantic.com/ideas/archive/2019/12/historians-clash-1619-project/604093/.

8 Serwer, "The Fight Over the 1619 Project Is Not About the Facts."

9 Serwer, "The Fight Over the 1619 Project Is Not About the Facts."

10 Serwer, "The Fight Over the 1619 Project Is Not About the Facts."

11 John G. Turner, "No One Year Can Unlock the Meaning of America," *National Review Online*, April 2, 2020, https://www.nationalreview.com/2020/04/new-york-times-1619-project-no-one-year-can-unlock-meaning-of-america/.

12 "Examining Slavery's Legacy with Nikole Hannah-Jones and Ibram X. Kendi," *Why Is This Happening? with Chris Hayes* (podcast and transcript), December 6, 2019, https://www.nbcnews.com/think/opinion/examining-slavery-s-legacy-nikole-hannah-jones-ibram-x-kendi-ncna1085646.

13 Dion J. Pierre and Peter W. Wood, *Neo-Segregation at Yale* (Princeton, NJ: National Association of Scholars, 2019).

POSTSCRIPT

1 Nikole Hannah-Jones on Twitter, @nhannahjones, July 27, 2020, https://twitter.com/nhannahjones/status/1287744904526012417.

2 "A Call for Reparations: How America Might Narrow the Racial Wealth Gap," Nikole Hannah-Jones interviewed by Terry Gross on *Fresh Air*, National Public Radio, June 24, 2020, https://www.npr.org/2020/06/24/882773218/a-call-for-reparations-how-america-might-narrow-the-racial-wealth-gap.

3 Rod Dreher, "What Is the 1619 Omelet?" *The American Conservative*, July 28, 2020, https://www.theamericanconservative.com/dreher/nikole-hannah-jones-1619-project-omelet/.

INDEX

Index

Index

Index

Index

Index

Index

Index

Index

Index

Index

Index

A NOTE ON THE TYPE

1620 *has been set in Baskerville, a family of types modeled after the work of English printer John Baskerville (1706–1775). Inspired by the example of William Caslon, Baskerville set out to produce the most perfect printing of his time, an endeavor that gave rise not only to a series of artistic successes, but also to noteworthy advancements on the technical side of printing. Baskerville's impact might have been limited in his homeland, but Giambattista Bodoni – a giant among Italian printers – was sufficiently impressed by his work to make an arduous pilgrimage to Birmingham to meet the ailing printer-typographer. ‡ The revival of Baskerville's types in the early twentieth century restored their creator's place in typographic history, even if some interpretations seem vastly less Baskervillean than others. Warm and inviting, yet not overly dark on the page, the Baskerville roman and italic are most successful at slightly larger text sizes. Their greater x-height and wider stance evince a distinct break with so-called old-style types of the seventeenth and eighteenth centuries and anticipate the work of Bodoni and Didot in the nineteenth.*

DESIGN & COMPOSITION BY CARL W. SCARBROUGH